TOUCHING THE LIGHT

To Nancy

you are truly a bright
shining light in this
world. May all that
you touch shine as bright
as you.

With much love

Keith

TOUCHING THE LIGHT

Keith Zang

iUniverse, Inc.
New York Lincoln Shanghai

TOUCHING THE LIGHT

Copyright © 2005 by Keith L. Zang

iUniverse books may be ordered through booksellers or by contacting:

iUniverse
2021 Pine Lake Road, Suite 100
Lincoln, NE 68512
www.iuniverse.com
1-800-Authors (1-800-288-4677)

ISBN: 0-595-32796-6

Printed in the United States of America

Dedicated to my wife, Enny
We had to travel half a world to find each other again.

Contents

Acknowledgments

To my family, Enny, Luna, and Mesa, who gave me the time and solitude to finish this book. To my extended family, my father, mother, brother Steve and his daughter Naomi, sisters Lisa, Jessica, Mary Ellen and her husband Joel and daughter Isabella, who at first thought I was a little crazy, but who are now discovering the path to their own sanity. To Enny's mother, Dina, in Indonesia who prayed for me every day and her father, Soewono, who helped us from his vantage point in the spiritual realm. To my stepparents, who have become part of our family and grandparents to my children, Sandi and Dan. A special thanks to my brother, Mark, who has been with us in spirit since before my physical birth, and to Michele, who has helped throughout the creation of this book with her varied talents and encouragement. Also to Randy and Terri Shaw, who showed me the doorway through which to walk, and Dr. Jim DeMeo, who opened many doors in my youth. Special thanks to all those who, in spirit, have aided my growth and healing in ways I never thought possible until they helped me remember. Finally, thanks to God for all that is.

Introduction

Light shines throughout the universe. This is not just the physical manifestation of light that we see when we turn on a lamp or look up at the stars. This light flows from the Creator and is a part of every one of us on this planet. Shining from within each of us is a bright light that cannot be extinguished. However, our internal light becomes dampened as we grow older and are filled with anxieties about paying bills, getting to our appointments on time, death, and the future. Our lives do not have to progress in that direction. We all have been given the tools to bring the light from within, out into our daily lives. It does not often happen spontaneously, but it will come forward through nurturing and seeking of knowledge.

Many people on this planet have begun, or shortly will begin, their search for the true meaning of their lives and their place within the universe. Each one of us holds a special place in relation to the cosmos, as we are each a spark and part of the Creator. As a part of the Creator, we have access to unlimited and unconditional energies. Discovering and using this energy can lead to a much fuller and healthier life. This book is one tool that will help bring forth knowledge that can be used to gain awareness of this abundance and to access it.

I have brought together several subjects under one book. Much of the knowledge presented here has been gained through personal experience and the help of dynamic and self-aware teachers and masters. I have used examples and experiences of real world people. I have combined theory with practice. Having a desire for change and a focus of direction will open the veil that separates our physical selves from our true, higher selves. As the veil of physical illusion drops away, the knowledge that everything is possible becomes clear.

Delving deeper into this book you will discover the paths to higher learning. You will learn about accessing the knowledge of ancient masters, conversing with loved ones that have crossed over, and feeling the kiss of angels. You will realize more about the incredible being that is you than you may have ever thought possible. The knowledge in this book is shared to help each person reading it remove the fears that stifle love for one another and ourselves. The fears that pervade this world come from feeling alone and isolated from the rest of God's creation. Reconnecting to the rest of the universe through our angels, loved ones, spirit guides, and knowledge of our past lives removes these fears and gives a greater sense of self. The universe is a place of unconditional love and acceptance. As we grow in knowledge about our true surroundings and ourselves, tapping into and touching the light is as simple as taking a breath.

"You can't wake a person that is pretending to be asleep"

—Native American Proverb

"When the student is ready, the teacher will appear"

—Buddhist Proverb

1

Standing on the First Brick of the Yellow Brick Road

Energy. Everything in the universe can be broken down into energetic particles. From the smallest atom to the largest galaxy, it is all made up of energy. This book consists of energetic particles moving around each other through mutual attraction and repulsion. Each person on this planet is made up of energy as well. From the thoughts in our heads to our beating hearts, everything that we are is made of energy. We are not as much the physical beings we think we are. All that surrounds us seems physical because of the underlying cohesion of the universe. It is held together by one major being, God. In knowing this, then all things in the universe are connected. This makes all things equal. The true person, the energetic being that exists beyond the physical that we see each morning in the mirror is connected to the universe and the universal consciousness. In becoming physical in this plane of existence, we forget our true selves and all that we are. In this knowledge lies the key to our own understanding. Each of us is as important to the universe as the largest galaxy. In earth and human societal relationships, each of us is as important as our country's leader. Each of us is as important as the richest and most powerful people on the planet are. This also goes for those we judge less important, such as homeless people we see on the street or those that are in prison for societal wrongs. We each have a different role to play while here on earth. As we delve deeper within ourselves and draw forward the universal consciousness that lies within each of us, this all becomes clear. That knowledge is part of all that is, all the way down to our DNA and chromosomal structure. Part of the learning and being here on earth is to rediscover this knowledge. In doing so, we learn and grow in ways that are far reaching not only for our own growth, but also for the growth of the universe as a whole.

Rediscovering this knowledge can take many forms. The difficulty in finding our true selves differs for each one of us. That is why it is important not to gauge ourselves and our progress against the accomplishments of others in this search. We are, each of us, at our own stages of development. We instead should focus on our progress and not be jealous or discouraged because another's seems more fruitful than our own. This is where balance comes in with our learning and growth. Being balanced is the key to making progress and enjoying the process. This can be difficult or easy depending upon how we choose to travel our individual path.

Often we are given an opportunity to see beyond the veil of our self-imposed reality. These moments give us a chance to take the experience and move forward with our development or to explain it away as a dream or a fluke of nature. Frequently we do not understand what happened to us, but it is the striving to know that is important. It keeps the doors of our perceptions open to further experiences. Some of us take this opportunity to look further into the possible cause of these occurrences. Others shrug them off as imagination or part of a dream. However, this is the dream. We are all dreaming and awaken when we cross back over into spirit. This is a realistic dream and has many physical laws that must be followed, but it is still a dream nonetheless.

As you read further in this book, I will share many private experiences that will help poke holes in this dream we live in and give a glimpse of a greater reality. Through years of study and direct experience, doorways have opened that have given me a larger picture of the world and universe around us. These are not experiences of mine alone but, through interaction with others, confirmations of this knowledge have occurred. Throughout this book, you will read how others have had the same experiences as me or have directly felt the impact of the work I have done with them. In some instances beliefs may be stretched. It is not my intention with this book to change the mind of each who reads it. I know every person reading these words has their own set of experiences and truths. The main goal of this book is to help those that are already on a spiritual path to confirm what they may have already experienced or to give new information to those that are searching for guidance on their own path. The doorways to our individual truths are right before us. All we have to do is reach out and turn the handle to open them.

This book is unique in that different subjects will be covered all in one book. Often many different books must be read to get the same information you will find in this one. I believe that all the subjects in this book flow together. It is the same with spiritual and self-discovery. As the doors open, information and ideas flow together to create a cohesive picture. The stories told here are unique but also represent what many people on this planet are experiencing. This book will give the reader much information in a small amount of space. I believe the time spent on spiritual discovery should be maximized. It is my intention that by the end of this book, the reader will have a greater understanding of a varied array of topics. This book will give information either to continue on a spiritual path with more tools or to aid in opening the minds of those just stepping through the doorway to their own self-awareness and discovery.

Before I get into the major subjects of this book, I think it is important to give a quick overview of my path of learning the techniques I now use and have taught to others and the circumstances and environment in which I have been able to accomplish much of what is covered throughout this book.

In 1998, I was opened to many new spiritual experiences after I learned Reiki, an energy healing technique. By 1999, I had become a Reiki master, as well as performed more than three hundred sessions in a clinic setting. I was working as the community health director for the Quinault Indian Nation in Taholah, Washington, a position I held for several years, after four years as the public works director. It was arranged with the clinic director that my Reiki teacher, Randy Shaw, and his wife, Terri, would come out twice a month, and we would do Reiki clinics to help those who wanted an alternative approach to their health care.

By 2000, my wife, Enny, and I purchased five acres in Washington state near Olympia and opened the Moonglow Enlightenment Center. I was still working for the Quinault Indian Nation, but we wanted to share our talents with others who needed healing, as well as teach all that we had been learning. This included energy healing, spiritual mediumship, and working with metaphysical energies on many different levels.

After learning Reiki from Randy Shaw, I began a journey of guided education and self-teaching for the next two years. Randy Shaw opened the doors to many new experiences and, through his guidance, I learned much very quickly. I also made sure to augment my studies with plenty of written material. One of my favorite authors, Ted Andrews, has produced a number of how-to books that helped both Enny and me to achieve a quick level of self-awareness and growth. We began reading books such as *Meet and Work with Spirit Guides, How to Uncover Your Past Lives, How To Heal with Color, The Healer's Manual, How to Do Psychic Readings Through Touch*, and other titles. I found his style easy to read and quickly informative. I began to read other books about meditation and incorporated it into my daily life. Through the spoken word and compact disks, I also was able to learn much through guided meditation as well as words of wisdom from many who already had traveled the path to true enlightenment. Some of these sages include Dr. Wayne Dyer, Thich Nhat Hanh, Dr. Andrew Weil, and Christopher Love. One book that truly inspired me was *Autobiography of a Yogi* by Paramahansa Yogananda. I quickly had lots of information stored within me, as well as plenty of opportunities to practice with people in many different situations. Always the student, I kept reading different books on astral travel, psychic development, stones and crystals, healing herbs, flower essences, and many other subjects, which I quickly incorporated into my practice. I not only learned via the written or spoken word, but I learned by doing, creating my own style and method of practice.

Moonglow became successful because of the unique items Enny and I put together to help others attain the same level of self-awareness we achieved. We began to do more teaching at Moonglow as well as reached out to many others online and through the phone. These connections became very successful as we never believed that time and space should be a barrier to growth. Many of the clients we worked with had very favorable outcomes. Their health improved, and they began to experience much of their own truths through their own levels of growth and enlightenment. We received confirmation after confirmation that what we were doing with others, and what they were doing with us, had validity. After each of our successes, our knowledge grew and our confidence was bolstered. Throughout much of this book, the work that Enny and I did with various clients, either in person or via distance, helps to emphasize different aspects of information or points I am conveying.

Enny and I searched for a community to express our growing spirituality and discovered Camp Edgewood, a spiritualist church near Tacoma, Washington. We began attending and were exposed to elders who had been working with metaphysical energies for years. Many grew up in a very actively spiritual environment and were eager to teach others the techniques and give opportunities to practice in a relaxed and open atmosphere. Enny and I took advantage of this, and we contributed to the services weekly with spiritual healing for the congregation, as well as doing intuitive readings for others. It was a wonderful hands-on experience in a caring and nurturing setting.

Desiring to share through the written word, I began to write articles on metaphysical subjects that were quickly picked up and published by various online publications. I also discovered the College of Metaphysical Studies, which offered online structured courses and degrees. I began a master's degree in Metaphysical Arts and was quickly asked to also teach because of my background and experience. It had all come easily for me; not because I possessed any special knowledge or skills other people did not have, but because since 1998 I dedicated myself twenty-four hours a day, seven days a week to spiritual discovery and self-aware-ness. It is like anything else, if a person spends the time and energy learning a skill, they will get good at it. Metaphysical Arts is the same way. The more a person studies and practices, the better they become at it. I want to stress that along with the personal study Enny and I have done over the years, many people have helped us along the way. We could not do it alone and are thankful to all who have helped. This was another motivation to write and share some of my own personal experiences and to help others along their path so they do not have to walk it alone.

One of the first experiences that hit home for me that what I was doing was real, had validity, and was extremely powerful was an instance in which I con-nected to one of the first spiritual mediums shortly after my awakening in 1998. The focus of this experience was with a friend of mine, Bill, who had crossed over into spirit in the late 1980s. The story needs to have a little history told behind it to give the full impact.

I was in high school on the South Side of Chicago in the late '70s and early '80s. There was an area of forest preserve very near my house that I and several other friends would visit on a regular basis. It was a chance for us to get away from the city environment and connect with a bit of natural energy that we always seemed to crave. One evening, Bill and I went to our regular spot to con-verse and talk about things that seemed important at the time. At one point Bill began to share with me how distressed he was becoming over the expectations of his family and himself. He had a lot of misgivings about his future and his ability to move forward with his life. He became so distraught that at one point he began to cry in total frustration and confusion. Being only seventeen, I shared with him words of advice and as much aid as I could, which seemed to help him out a lot. We did not speak again of that evening and, in fact, I had forgotten about it totally.

Bill went on to join the Navy and became a fighter pilot, flying F-14s from an aircraft carrier. He became one of the best in his class and was considered a "Top Gun." He eventually married and had children. His marriage soon became very unhappy, and his desire to stay in the Navy as a pilot began to wane. He trans-ferred to the Marines and began flying Apache helicopters in the hopes of bring-ing something different to his life. Bill and I were both very different people. His was a life of war, mine of peace. By the time Desert Shield came along in 1990, I was in the Peace Corps in Papua New Guinea. I did not know it at the time, but I was a source of inspiration for Bill to get out of the military and do something different with his life. He would not get the chance. Bill was killed in his Apache helicopter rescuing downed fighter pilots in Iraq during Desert Shield.

I received the news soon after I returned from Papua New Guinea in late 1990. I was saddened but not surprised, as I knew Bill was in the middle of the war. Soon after he crossed into spirit, he began to come to my dreams. He was never overtly involved in the dreams but would be more in the periphery, sitting and watching. Often I would go to him in my dreams and talk to him, say hello, and ask him questions about how he was doing. I was not psychically "in tune" then, but I knew it was him communicating with me, letting me know that he was OK.

In 1998, I connected with a medium online that was very open and well versed in bridging to the spiritual realms. Bill was one of the first people with whom I connected. The medium, who called herself Star, quickly linked to Bill. She relayed the information about the day that Bill and I were in the Chicago forest preserve and the impact it had on him. She described the scene perfectly down to the path we were on and the surrounding area. He relayed through her that he was at the point of taking his own life and that the words I spoke to him that evening convinced him otherwise. He wanted to thank me for the time I spent with him and the encouragement that he received.

After hearing those words from him, I was taken aback. Not only had I completely forgotten about the incident, because it had occurred eighteen years before, but I had no idea of the true significance of that evening. After comprehending the importance of what was being relayed to me, I truly felt the impact of that time we spent together. I held out my hands, palms upward, and asked Bill to come forward and place his hands on mine. I instantly felt his presence and the tingling energy of his hands on my own. I soon realized I had tears of joy/sadness running down my face. I intuitively knew that Bill felt the same, and this fact was soon relayed by Star. This was my first real experience with spiritual connecting on not only a higher plane, but also in connecting on the physical plane as well. This incident touched me deeply not only because of the connection with Bill, but because Star had done this session without me present or ever meeting me in person. I knew then that time and space were not an issue and, if I studied hard and put my heart into it, I would be able to do the same for others.

I have been blessed to have many experiences before and after those few moments with Bill and Star. They were powerful enough to help me continue my path on a more focused course. Many other instances that had very powerful effects on me helped lead up to my spiritual opening in 1998. Like so many other people that experience these types of events, I was very unsure what to make of them. This is also true for many people that go through life not aware that the world and universe around them is alive with unperceived sentient energies that take many forms and create seemingly unexplainable circumstances. Most often, these occurrences happen when we are younger, but we remember them throughout our lifetimes. These seemingly bizarre instances are glimpses into the true reality beyond our delusional perceptions of life. They are the proverbial carrot on a stick that is offered to us to delve deeper. Because we are so focused on the tasks and environments at hand, we do not see the larger picture. Very few people look outward from themselves, let alone outward to the cosmos, and realize there is much more going on than our limited perceptions can perceive. There is activity around us all the time. A simple example is the air we breathe. It is an important aspect of our lives. Without it, there would be no physical life on this planet. It is all around us, moving and mixing as we inhale in and out. The air is quite dense and heavy compared to the vacuum of space. We notice this heaviness most often when wind blows. In extreme instances, the wind causes damage to the human and natural environments. However, wind also can create energy, cool us on hot days, and push clouds around to move rain. We don't see it but, because mankind has studied it and now has a better understanding of it, physical laws can be applied, thus making wind a less mystical force.

It is the same with the spirit worlds. They are around us all the time. We are an integral part of these worlds because we are spirit ourselves, only in a more substantial and physical form. Most people are not attuned to those energies because of their physical, world-minded focus. With learning and study, the channeling of energy for healing, as well as communicating with spiritual energies, becomes known and understood by those taking the time. Spending this time to learn gives us a chance to relearn that which we lost through our birth into physical form. Spiritual energies are often silent, working unseen, yet are an important part of our lives. Like air, they are not noticed until they blow, like the wind, for us to feel. When spiritual energies make us take notice, we wake up to acknowledge the existence of something most people are unable to perceive. Spiritual energies usually do not make themselves known unless there are circumstances that require their assistance. Then they are momentarily apparent to intervene on our behalf or to help us in ways that cannot be explained by the physical laws of known science.

Once we are ready to move forward with our spiritual growth, then teachers imparting various forms of information will begin to come our way. Many doors will open to further our understanding of the world and the greater universe around us. Change may occur slowly or, as in many cases, quickly. That change occurs within us not with the world or universe as a whole. The information that lies beyond our own self-imposed veils has always been there, but our perceptions may not have been able to comprehend its existence as a reality. However, it does exist, and it is vast and wondrous.

There were two experiences in my late teens and early twenties that began to open the doors for me into understanding there was more to the physical world I perceived. I was not sure what had occurred at the time or where to go for answers, but the doors to change were opened, and it was just a matter of time before they would swing wider to give me a better view.

The first incident involved a trip in the summer of 1982. Bryan, a friend of mine since high school, and I decided to go to a concert in Alpine Valley, Wisconsin to see Neil Young, a rock and roll performer. Alpine Valley was a ski resort in the winter and a concert venue in the summer. We stayed for the show until late in the evening, and then began the drive back to Beloit where Bryan was attending college. It was a dark four-lane highway with a large grass median between the oncoming lanes and ours. As Bryan and I were talking about whatever it was that seemed important at the time, out of the darkness appeared a car that was ditched in the grassy median but was more than half in our lane. It had no lights on, either headlights or hazard lights, and was in our path. I knew that we were going to hit it going 65 miles an hour. It was at that point time seemed to slow down to a crawl. The car was no longer rushing to meet us but seemed to be moving slower. I turned the wheel sharply, and then everything began to happen in slow motion. We avoided the collision and, the moment we were out of danger, time began to speed up again until it was back to normal. Based on the laws of physics, the distance we had to turn and the speed at which we were traveling, there was no way we should have missed hitting that car which, by the time we were aware of it, was more than halfway into our lane. Time slowed down to allow me to react and get our vehicle out of harm's way.

Bryan and I looked at each other in shock.

"Did what I think happen really just happen?" I asked.

"I think so," Bryan said, equally dumbfounded.

We drove on in silence for twenty minutes or so going over the event repeatedly in our heads. I kept seeing the car in front of us, time slowing down, and then us missing the vehicle. I broke the silence and "replayed" aloud what had just happened and what I had seen. He said he had experienced the same things. We tried to analyze what had happened from our limited perspectives. Was it our perception? Did time slow down to allow us to miss that car? Was the car an illusion? We just did not know. The only thing we were sure of was that something unusual, which we could not explain, had occurred.

Much later in life, I began to understand that time is not constant. It can be slowed down or accelerated. It is another part of our illusion and is fixed only in relation to the person who is experiencing it. We, as human beings, are three-dimensional. Taking into account the past and what we know of the future, we perceive time as a constant flow. As we get away from our third dimensional existence, however, we lose that sense of the passage of time. There is only "now" and "what is." Many of the more ascended masters that have taught down through the ages have mastered the concept of living for the moment and have tried to impart that knowledge to the general populace. Often existing in the moment is something that needs to be learned, as we are always ready to admonish ourselves for something we did or should have done, thus tying us to our past that seems to return to haunt us. The future is an insubstantial thing that keeps us desiring for something better, thus creating a situation where we do not appreciate what we have in our present. The constant striving for change and "greener grass" keeps us always wishing for the future to become our present. Westernized society is addicted to this, as people are always looking for the new and improved version of what they are using.

The future is also something that is ever changing. Few people on this planet have been able to foretell future events. That is because each of us has free will. We can change our future with the decisions we make. There are probable futures given the path we are going down or the desires that we will make manifest in our lives. We have certain life purposes that we continually are being drawn to, but there are few absolutes in terms of future events. We are each given the gift of free will to shape and mold our lives. There also are societal issues that may hamper or block some of our attempts to create the life we want. These are hurdles to be overcome. As we get past the blocks in our life, we not only learn and grow in the process, but also get closer to our life's goal and purpose.

I have learned by connecting with many spiritual beings that are not limited by third dimensional constraints that living in the present is much more rewarding and healthier than living in the past or always striving for the future. In addition, once the time/space barrier is overcome, anything is possible. By removing limiting beliefs and concepts from our lives, we remove the ideas that our environment and our weaknesses limit us. It is through our environment and our seeming weaknesses that we are able to overcome our limitations to do the impossible, thus bringing the realization that all things are possible.

The second instance that occurred during my college years was in 1987, several months before completing my course of studies at Illinois State University and graduating. I was living in an apartment with my then-girlfriend, Marti. I was in our bathroom, about to put up a Beck's beer sign to adorn our palatial student apartment. This beer sign was made of plastic and was used as a promotional item in liquor stores. A friend who was working in a liquor store had given me the sign. This was an extra sign that was not going to be used by the store-owner. It was a thicker sign that would protrude from the wall. It also had a small hole in the back where it had been damaged from transport but would be hidden from sight once it was hung. I had the hammer and nails out, ready to do the complex task of hanging the sign, when Marti informed me it was time to go meet some friends for lunch. So, I put the sign down on the floor and left it to finish the job when we returned.

Several hours later, we returned to the apartment. I went back to the bathroom and picked the sign up. It was still in the same place I had left it, but it was different. It was still the green Beck's beer sign, but it was not the same. The one I now held in my hands was thinner, much thinner. I turned it over to see if the hole was still in the back, but that also had changed. It was gone. I turned the sign over and over in my hands, trying to figure out what was going on. I thought I might have had two signs the same, and this one was switched, but I knew that I only had one. I had a strange "Twilight Zone" feeling that everything had somehow changed. I went over to Marti and asked her the date and the year, as if that somehow had changed. Everything was, of course, the same, except the sign. I once again thought of the car incident with Bryan and knew I was again in an inexplicable situation that was turning my world upside down. I knew something extraordinary had happened, but I could not quite figure out what it was or the significance of it. Why would something as unimportant as a cheap plastic beer sign become so important and life changing? I was perplexed and had no way at that point in time to figure it out. I knew there was an important message being shown to me but, with my limited understanding and abilities, it was impossible to know what it was.

Now that I have grown older and wiser, the reason for the beer sign change was told to me by several of my spirit guides. They said they had done it as a practical joke. From their viewpoint, it was something funny. However, from my viewpoint at that time, it was something short of a miracle. They chose the beer sign as a symbol. At that point in my life, I was a busy bartender and college student. I still enjoyed drinking beer and when I wasn't working or studying, I was out at a local bar or at a college party. They knew it would be something I would notice and, in noticing it, I again would reflect on the nature of the universe and my reality. To them, it was a simple matter of changing the physical nature of the sign. To me, it was something serious that shook my world.

I had two other experiences in 1987 and 1988 that also were of equal importance in keeping my eyes open to a more spiritual path. In 1987, I spent my last summer of college in South Dakota, completing an internship with the Indian Health Service. For three months, I worked professionally with a mentor to help me strengthen my skills and knowledge in my chosen field of environmental health. It was time to take all that I had learned in college and put it into practice. When the opportunity came, I jumped on it. It was a chance for me to get out of Illinois, and into the beautiful state of South Dakota. At the time, I thought it was just coincidence and happening at the right time, but now I know it was the many American Indian spirit guides that I have had with me for many years that led me there. They helped orchestrate my internship so I would be in a place that would optimize my learning and experiences to help carry me down the path I was to make my professional specialty, environmental health with indigenous peoples.

The work was not only science-oriented, but also people-oriented. It was science put into practice. Public health work is preventative in nature. The philosophy is if conditions are kept in such a manner that injuries and illness can be eliminated through sanitary and safe practices, then medical care and the subsequent pain and suffering that goes with it can also be greatly reduced. This is accomplished through engineering controls of environments to make them safe and ensuring safe food handling and potable water, separating sewage from the living environment, and implementing other strategies to keep disease-carrying vectors and situations from occurring. Unfortunately, due to our disconnectedness from nature and ourselves, we as humans break all the rules and create unsafe and unsanitary conditions, thus perpetuating illnesses, diseases, and human suffering.

The Yankton and Santee Sioux reservations where I lived were no different in many ways to other rural communities in terms of their health needs, but they were different in other ways due to their background and history as American Indian people. Not many economic opportunities existed for community members, and the transition from being a proud, independent group of people until the mid-1800s to the modern day group they were in the late 1980s still had a great impact on each person. There was a lot of depression and desire for change without the mechanism to help make it happen. Outwardly, the people were friendly and, in most cases, helpful, and my learning experiences were deep and meaningful. The three months I spent helped me greatly move from a college environment to a professional one.

One instance shone through the third dimensional life I was leading into the spiritual, but it was brief. I attended two different powwows organized by the local tribes. There was a lot of preparation leading up to these events, and the people were proud of the various roles they played in making it happen. By pow-wow standards, they were not overly large, but the importance they played in the community was tremendous. Many dancers throughout the two-day event dressed up in their finest traditional outfits that were dazzling to the eye. Watching the people dance was quite an experience. There was a lot of true spirituality in what they did. I did not know it at the time, but the connection between their spirit guides, animal totems, and the dancers was extremely powerful. Some of the dancers became lost in their dancing and this connection. It was something that I did not see, but many of the community people knew and understood. Some people would dance for hours in the hot sun, filled with the energy of spirit and oblivious to the weight of the flesh. It was truly a remarkable sight.

During these powwows, I experienced spending some time in tepees. Several people brought tepees to the gathering. Two were used to serve food, and several were used for lodging and gathering during the ceremonies. Men sat around and socialized in one of these tepees. It was much cooler in the tepee than outside, so it was an optimal place to get away from the heat of the day. It smelled like dirt, grass, canvas, and people. I looked up at the tall tip where the poles joined, and then around at the shape and traditional feel of it. I was instantly in love.

I knew one of the men in the tepee from the hospital I was based out of, and he asked me to come in for a while and talk with a group of men gathered inside. We discussed local happenings, some information about me, and my life plans after leaving their area, and they shared information about themselves. They introduced me to a local medicine man, and I told him some of my experiences and interests with natural healing. We talked for a while about these matters without him sharing much information about himself. I did most of the talking, and him most of the listening. After a while it was time for me to go, but before I left he looked me deep in the eyes and told me I would be working with great energies and going places both physically and spiritually that would lead me down a path of great knowledge. I did not know how to respond to that. I felt a great surge of tingling energies go down my back. I thanked him and the other men in the tepee and walked back out into the bright and hot sunlight. I was perplexed yet filled with the idea of a bright future. I still had many years to travel before fully realizing that man's prophecy.

After my three-month internship, I returned to Chicago and began to look for work associated with my chosen field. Indian Health Service offered me a chance to work with them, but the paperwork would take several months. In the meantime, I needed to find work. I had been a waiter and bartender throughout my college years, so I decided to take up that profession again. It was in this transitional time that another spiritual experience happened to me.

It was in a restaurant in the Old Town area of Chicago on Wells Street. It was an Italian restaurant just down the street from Second City and Zany's comedy clubs. Upstairs used to be a candy shop where the owner had become despondent and hung himself in the middle of the store several years earlier. As I started work, it was relayed to me that the building was haunted. I always believed in ghosts and was eager to have a sighting or some type of experience. I was not to be disappointed.

Two swinging saloon-type doors separated the main kitchen area from the customer area. Several times during my shifts, they would be pushed forward and then swing back as if someone was walking through them, but there was no one visible. At night after closing when we would be cleaning up, we could hear footsteps upstairs, but we knew there was no one up there. The restaurant had a motion detector that was used as an alarm that would constantly go off. There also was a tape deck upstairs that played continuous cassettes for ambient music. It would mysteriously turn off. The company that serviced the machines inspected it and found no defects. I usually was the one who volunteered to go upstairs to turn it back on. Everyone else was too frightened to go up alone, but I always had hoped to see the man as a ghostly apparition floating through the air. However, I never did see him fully in that manner.

One of the dishwashers told me a story of his experience with our spiritual resident. One evening the garbage can into which table scraps were dumped suddenly fell over as though an unseen force had pushed it. The garbage cans were extremely heavy. It took at least two strong men to move and empty them each night, but that evening the can tipped over as if it were empty.

The final story from this restaurant happened one February evening around 11:30 PM when six waiters, including me, were leaving for the night. I looked up at a circular upstairs window and saw the face of a man looking out. When the others looked up, they too saw the man who then disappeared as quickly as he had appeared. We all knew it was our spiritual inhabitant, and the incident was the topic of conversation for the next couple of weeks.

I know now that this man who had taken his own life was a spirit trapped between the worlds. Although he was no longer in physical form, he had not yet moved into the light of higher vibration that some call heaven. I have often found this to be true in cases of suicide. Unable or unwilling to walk into the gateway to the light to begin their healing process, the person finds him or herself trapped in the very physical environment from which they were trying to escape. They become angry and despondent. It is during these times when physical phenomena, such as pushing over garbage cans or wandering through the premises with no purpose, can occur. If the spirit is unaware that they have not yet moved out of their physical bodies, they may become angry when we can neither see nor understand them. They become known as poltergeists and tend to throw things or move objects around the room. They are not necessarily evil, just frustrated.

To help these spiritual energies move on, someone of higher vibration must intervene on his or her behalf. Alternatively, a group of people might get together and pray for the person, letting them know that they have crossed over into spirit and that it is all right for them to walk into the light. Lighting white candles and asking angels to help show them the way also will help those trapped in the physical world to move into the light of God's love and healing energies.

At that time though, I was unaware of these issues. I just knew I was in the middle of a haunted restaurant and enjoyed the thrill of it. I since have learned to help those who have been trapped as will be relayed later in this book. But the main impression left upon me was that, indeed, there are spiritual presences around us, and those several months left me no doubts as to the existence of our souls after physical death. However, I still had not been able to connect the incident to being able to connect to the spiritual realms yet.

It would be many years before my spiritual medium skills would come to the forefront and, in the meantime, many other experiences were needed to prepare myself to be mature enough to be able to handle the responsibility of speaking and passing messages from those in the higher realms of existence to those present on earth.

2

The Ever-Changing Permanence of Western Science

Science is a wonderful thing. It can help to explain the laws that we are made to obey on planet earth. Physics is the biggest one to which we are tied. Rate of movement, weight, time, etc. are concepts we all understand or at least have some nominal knowledge. Traveling to a place on earth going a certain speed will get us there in a certain amount of time. We continually have pushed the envelope of speed and travel, starting with domestication of animals and harnessing the power of rivers and streams to the steam engine, internal combustion engine, jets, and now rockets. It is all about harnessing energy to modify what we were not given at birth. Our legs can carry us only so far, but our minds continue to develop modes of travel to physically take us farther and faster.

Chemistry is another. The way our bodies integrate food, air, and water are all tied to chemical processes. When the body begins to get out of balance due to stresses, emotional or physical traumas, or long-term abuse through bad diet, lack of exercise, and constant fear, those chemical processes begin to go awry causing physical ailments. Pure Western science tries to put that balance back through chemistry, working on a physical level and ignoring many other aspects of our being, such as the emotional and spiritual.

Pure science is lacking in many areas, because much of scientific theory has been taken as fact. The area of metaphysics goes beyond the physical definition of time and space and works on a much higher plane. Balancing these two can be tricky and has caused many problems throughout the ages for those doing the balancing. Christian saints have had a tough time of it. They have been hapless victims of misunderstanding, fear, and political intrigue, which, for them, was often fatal. But looking at many of the stories of saints, whether Christian, Hindu, Buddhist, or other major faiths, gives us great insight into the study of metaphysics, as well as glimpses into what we can become if we step out of our

15

scientific boxes and look at a more broad view of the world and potential around us.

Many are the stories of Hindu saints that were and are able to instantaneously transport themselves from one place to another, or they were seen in two or more places at the same time. Others have been able to pull from thin air food, clothing, and other items to help those in need. Many instances have been documented through history of the possibilities that can be accomplished when tied into the unlimited resources the Creator has provided for us. However, much of past and modern science has discounted or flat out ignored many of these happenings throughout time or has worked to discredit the action as well as the person that is accomplishing it. In some cases, it has led to direct persecution. I have had some experience in this realm. It was a catalyst to begin to step out of the scientific community that I was immersing myself in and look at the broader picture. I was given a view of a complete alternative to Western science, which got me involved in a wider view of healing and health itself. I tell this story to help encourage all people to look beyond what is seen as "scientific," thus valid. What we know now and praise as true over time can be seen as antiquated or just a plain mistake.

In 1983, during the beginning of my fourth semester of study at Illinois State University, a light began to shine in me. I was taking my required courses as I began a path in the business field. One of the classes offered was physical geography-how earthquakes happen, how rain is made, and other aspects of our planet. I envisioned it being another boring class where an old tenured professor talked to us about the makeup of the planet in a monotone voice, putting half the class to sleep. I was wary of this after I had taken an astronomy class. I thought it would be exciting as we talked about far off galaxies and the solar system and looked through telescopes. It ended up being physics and lots of math, which I barely squeaked through.

This class turned out to be a mind-awakening experience because of the professor, Dr. James DeMeo. He was an interesting and dynamic speaker. He awakened in me a spirit for change. He not only talked about the physical aspects of the planet, but he also was an activist that talked about all of the problems we were facing environmentally. He talked about Love Canal, New York, where chemicals were leaching into people's drinking water and causing major health problems. We discussed the hazards of nuclear power and the alternatives of wind, solar, and biomass. We talked about agriculture and pesticides in our food. Many of these things I was unaware of, but I soon became an activist for change. I started to go to the library and read as much as I could about alternative energy, food additives, natural diets, extinction of animals, and an array of many other subjects. I was largely self-educated. The transformation was quick and decisive. By the next semester, I had changed my major to environmental health. It turned out that Illinois State University had one of the best environmental health programs in the country. The problem was I had to start all over again, taking many of the hard sciences such as chemistry, physics, and anatomy. The next semester I enrolled with a full load of science-oriented classes.

It was a hard road the next two years. I was in a limbo state. I was not able to begin work in my major field of study, yet I already had completed most of the required courses from ISU. The hard science courses were difficult and time-consuming because of the extra labs that were a part of them. I already had gone to school for two years, and I was looking forward to something that would be more practical. This came in the form of my minor area of study, geography. For the next two years, I took four more courses with Dr. DeMeo. They were the fuel for my internal fire. Dr. DeMeo became my mentor. I looked up to him throughout those years. His classes were exciting and radical for the school and the department in which he was teaching. Many of his colleagues looked down on him and thought of him as a troublemaker. He did not teach the same as his peers. Instead of tests, he would have everyone write one major paper that would make up the bulk of the grade. During the course, the students would have to figure out the time of the full moon, which was when an update or progress report of their area of interest relating to the course would be due. These were called "Moonthly Reports." Many students did not understand this process and wanted the regular tests to measure their progress of learning. However, Dr. DeMeo wanted the students to think independently and have responsibility for their own learning. He also wanted them to be more aware of their natural surroundings. At the beginning of each course, I would hear several students protest, and by the next class there were fewer students. Once students began to understand how much easier it was and how much more they would learn, the class was a lively environment in which to scholastically grow.

After the first semester with Dr. DeMeo, I began to learn about his research on Dr. Wilhelm Reich's work with Orgone energy. Born in Austria in 1897, Dr. Reich began to work with life force energies that he termed "Orgone energies." By the 1930s, he was building devices called "Orgone Accumulators," which were conduits for life force energy. Basically, these were boxes built from organic materials, such as wood, as well as metallic components such as steel wool. A person sitting in them for a specified time would absorb large quantities of healing, life force energies. Through this absorption, wonderful benefits would occur. As he worked with this energy, he began to see dramatic results. At this same time, he developed his "Cloud Buster." This was a device built from long tubes set on a trailer. A flexible pipe in the back would be placed into a body of energetic water such as a pond. When pointed at a small cumulus cloud, the cloud would break it up within minutes. The practical application of the Cloud Buster was during drought conditions. When used in a specified manner, an energetic environment was created whereby rain clouds would form. Within forty-eight to seventy-two hours, there would be vast quantities of precipitation.

Dr. Reich moved to the United States in 1939 but by the early and mid-1950s, he was under attack by the Western medical establishment and the FDA. In 1955, he was imprisoned for transporting an unregulated medical device (Orgone accumulator) over state lines. By 1957, he crossed over into spirit while in prison. Many of his books were burned, and he and his works were labeled dangerous and his theories a menace to Western society. This was a very clear instance in history of direct persecution of one man due to his different views.

It was Dr. Reich's theories that Dr. DeMeo was attempting to prove. He had conducted successful cloud-busting experiments in Florida and Kansas. He had built a large Cloud Buster and was trying to get mainstream science to take notice of the validity and the incredible usefulness of all the devices on which Dr. Reich had worked. Unfortunately, no one at Illinois State would pay any attention. In fact, the physicists and others in the science community slandered and maligned Dr. DeMeo without even meeting him or facing him in private, let alone in public. I remember an evening when Dr. DeMeo put together a presentation of his work after a particularly scathing article in the local paper was written about him and his work. He had slides, graphs, and lots of information on his research and results. Few people showed up. The audience consisted primarily of those who were supportive of his work. That evening I learned much about the clique that Western science had become and is now a reality in the third millennium. The views that Dr. DeMeo expressed were scorned by his peers because they did not understand them nor did they want to. I learned a valuable lesson that evening about the status quo, and I continually face those same challenges as I write this book.

After several years, Dr. DeMeo was asked to leave Illinois State University because of his differing views. He ultimately moved to Oregon where he founded the Biophysical Research Laboratory outside of Ashland. He also was hired by several countries, such as Greece, Israel, and Namibia, where he conducted successful cloud-busting operations that ended severe drought conditions in those regions.

Dr. DeMeo and I are doing work that is two sides of the same coin when it comes to healing with life force energies, but our paths are quite a bit different. He is working to scientifically prove the existence and value of life force energies through rigorous testing, experimentation, and documentation. It is important for the scientific community to understand the value of using these energies for the betterment of all people on this planet. His path follows an empirical one. Mine, on the other hand, is one that is more intuitive in nature and does not rely as rigorously on scientific means. Much of the path I follow does not require the need for scientific proof, but more in trusting that life force energy, the value in its utilization and the power that it can bring for healing, is an innate and intrinsic part of life itself. The fact that we are here and alive is, to me, proof enough of its existence. However, both of our viewpoints are important to humankind's understanding and utilization of these energies on a regular basis in whatever form. Although Dr. DeMeo is not associated in any way with the work I am now doing, I believe that in terms of teaching others about a softer approach to healing, we are on a parallel course. Each of us is using completely different means. I know that someday soon those in the scientific and mainstream medical communities will see the value of the work that people like Dr. DeMeo are doing.

The main ideas that were imparted on me by being exposed to Dr. DeMeo's and Dr. Reich's work was that there is much out there that is not understood by mainstream science. At the time that I was taking hard core science classes, I realized that most of what I was studying were theories that were just as unproven as Dr. Reich's but had more acceptance. I began to recognize that the strands that were holding our view of the world as seen through the glasses of our current scientific understanding could be dramatically altered by understanding the nature of life force energy, the connectedness of all living things, and our connection with the universe at large. As I lived these moments in time through my college years, I began to see beyond what was presented to me, knowing that there is still much out there to be explored and understood.

In our modern times, the nature of science is changing each time a person does a Reiki or other type of hands-on healing session with another person, especially in a clinical setting. The medical community, which in the past has followed rigorous procedures, is now opening up to understand that health is more than just giving a pill or using radiation on a diseased part of the body. Many hospitals and health centers are integrating a holistic approach to health, which ultimately translates into the science of health and health care. Intangible ideas, such as having the patient in a positive state of mind or using creative visualization to build up immunity and healing, is now finding its way into the healing regimen. Patients also are taking their health into their own hands learning ancient techniques such as meditation and yoga. The plant kingdom is being seen as valuable as people are turning to medicinal herbs as well as raw, organically grown fruits and vegetables. General awakening is occurring in Westernized society that for several hundred years has been lost in the drive to understand the mechanistic workings of our minds, bodies, physical environment, and even our souls. In this great awakening, many people are realizing that there is no separation between their physical selves and the rest of the universe. It is all connected, and each and every aspect of our world, the universe, and ourselves is one in the same. The energy that flows through all things and has created all things comes from one source, God. Tapping into this unlimited source of energy can change a person's perspective and life for the better.

3

Can I Get Some Healing Energies with that Band-Aid?

For many people, the road toward enlightenment can be a long one. Often we need many experiences to open the doorways to the path that will be our ultimate life purpose. Many people that I have met have worked their way through or in conjunction with Western medicine in some form or another. This even includes those that have suffered long or severe illnesses and have spent time in hospitals or with many visits to the doctor. It helps to develop empathy and a desire to help others through their illnesses, whether physical or emotional. It also can bring a desire to help on a deeper level, one that Western medicine often cannot accomplish in the absence of integration with other healing modalities. The limitations of Western medicine can bring frustration to those that work or attempt to heal within its confines, bringing a desire to learn more and varied ways of healing. I have followed this path for many years. After working in South Dakota, I joined the U.S. Peace Corps in 1988 and was sent to Papua New Guinea (PNG). PNG is just above Australia, at the beginning of the South Pacific and the tail end of Southeast Asia. At the time I was there, it was still a fairly traditional place, with many remote areas of people not accustomed to outsiders interacting with them. There were still a lot of traditional beliefs surrounding health and the spirit world, but Westernized medicine also was widely practiced. I was entering this world as a health and nutrition educator, and it was my job to bring Western scientific knowledge to help with overall nutritional status, particularly when it came to children. There was still a twenty-five percent infant mortality rate, some of it due to traditional beliefs about the health and well-being of children as well as the nutritional value of some of the foods that were eaten on a regular basis.

I started the first few weeks in a town called Goroka. It is a city in the Highlands region of the country that enjoys fertile soils and an abundance of fruits and vegetables grown from seeds imported from throughout the world. The weather was mild with an abundance of rainfall. Nutritionally, the people were healthy but suffered from many other ailments known throughout the world. I spent the first week in Goroka at the local hospital to observe their healthcare system in action.

The first few minutes of the first day I arrived, I was placed in the obstetrics and nursery ward. As I entered, a nurse was giving artificial respiration with a bag mask to a newborn baby. Within a few minutes of watching them, she asked me if I wanted to help. Nervously, I agreed and before I knew it, I was giving artificial respiration to a newborn infant. I had never done it before, and I was a little hesitant. As I held the small baby with one hand and arm and gently squeezed air into the tiny lungs with the bag mask, the nurse explained to me this baby born in the bush had stopped breathing shortly after birth. The family brought the newborn in, and the hospital staff was going through the motions for the parents. The baby had quit breathing for quite a while before it was brought into the hospital, and the prognosis was not good. The heart was still barely beating, so they attempted resuscitation. I gave the baby CPR for about fifteen minutes before the heart finally quit beating altogether. They took the baby from my arms, wrapped it in the towel it came in, and gave it back to the parents for burial. The parents were saddened but thanked me in their humble way for the work I had done. I did not feel like a hero. It was strange, but throughout the whole experience, I felt a kind of detachment. There were so many changes and new things being thrown at me, it was hard to take it all in at once.

That same day in the same area, another infant that was only several days old was being prepared for surgery. When it was born, it had an unformed twin attached to its body. They let me hold the baby and examine the twin. It was not fully developed, so many of the things that would define a human being were not there. It was more like a dark mass growing on the lower left abdominal area. Vague outlines of legs and arms as if in a fetal position were visible but not much else. The next day I saw the baby, and there was a white gauze bandage where the twin had been.

One experience each of us went through at the hospital was being present during the birth of a baby. The birth I was to witness that day was a cesarean. It was a new experience for me. Another volunteer in our group, Wanda, was with me throughout the day and also was to be present during the operation. They put us into surgical clothing over our other clothing. The oddest thing, though, was that everyone went in with bare feet. There we all were, dressed up, scrubbed up, and in bare feet. It was a situation that to me was quite comical. However, this being my first time in an operating room about to be witness to a C-section, I was unfamiliar with the procedure.

We all assembled around the patient as the anesthetic was administered, and she slowly lost consciousness. The scar on her abdomen proclaimed she had been through a cesarean before. The doctor began by cutting through the scar tissue. I had never seen an operation up close, and to me it was fascinating. The scar tissue was white but, as the incision bled, became red. After several moments, the initial cut through the scar tissue had been made, and the deeper incisions that would ultimately lead to the uterus began. It did not take long before an incision long enough and wide enough to bring the baby out was completed. The infant was quickly extracted and brought into the world. It took about ten seconds and, after suctioning the mouth, she soon began to wail and cry, which was a great sound to our ears. The doctor looked up at the both of us and asked if either one of us wanted to cut the cord. Wanda declined, so I stepped forward and did the honors. I really enjoyed that moment of participation. The baby was cleaned up and placed under a warmer, because the operating room was kept cool. It then was time to close the incision, which took only a few minutes. The whole process took about an hour from the time we dressed for the operating room to the time the finishing stitches were completed.

Midway through the cesarean, I noticed another operating room adjoined to the one where we were. People had filed in to perform another surgical procedure. I could not see what was occurring but stole glances over there once in a while. I asked one of the nurses what procedure was going on next to us, but she told me in a muffled voice I could not understand. I still felt as though I did not belong due to my feelings of inexperience, so I did not ask again, pretending I understood.

By the time everything was completed in our operating theater, I requested permission to go and observe the other procedure. The head nurse said it was perfectly OK and to feel free to stay as long as I wanted. I moved next door and began to view the next operation. It was more than I had expected. They had a man on the table, just opened up, and the doctor, a man from India wearing a turban, was in the middle of removing the man's small intestines and placing them on top of his abdomen. As I entered, several people looked up and noticed me, somewhat questioningly, so I explained briefly that I was over participating in the other room and then asked if it was OK to observe the current procedure. The surgeon happily welcomed me, as more intestines were taken out of the man's abdominal cavity. I was amazed at the quantity of intestines that were removed, because it seemed like an endless supply kept coming. After a while, he stopped pulling them out and then brought out what I now know as the liver. I stood quietly and watched. Before too long the operation was completed. I returned to the locker room to change clothes and went home.

I had never been in an operating room before, and it was quite an experience. As a training tool, it gave me the chance to observe a process that has become the norm in Western medicine. Too often, doctors are willing to cut someone open to get at the cause of the disease rather than take the time and effort to work with the body's own healing mechanisms. For many doctors, this is all that they know. Granted, there are circumstances in which surgery is necessary, but it should be the treatment of last resort rather than the first. Witnessing the surgeries in the Goroka Hospital was my first of many such episodes throughout my career in Western medicine. However, the two I viewed for the first time touched me most deeply.

For several days, I stayed at the hospital and worked in different wards to the best of my ability. This education was to help us in the future when we would be out in the villages with only an aid post, which was the most basic health care available in the remote areas. It would be little more than basic first aid and sometimes not even that if there were no supplies available. Therefore, I learned how to bandage, give shots, and experience first hand various maladies that would be encountered. Some of the more frequent were malaria, ringworm, scabies, pneumonia, burns, and anemia. There also was still a fair amount of polio throughout the country. It was not uncommon to see someone walking with a stick with one healthy leg and one leg too thin to support the weight. Many of the diseases and conditions that were present in PNG were not nearly as prevalent in the U.S. It was a different set of circumstances, so I spent as much time and effort possible gathering information and learning important aspects of health and health care. I knew it would all come in handy when I left Goroka and was sent to my permanent posting.

After spending the next eight weeks in various forms of training including language and culture, I was sent to a town called Kiunga in a remote area in the southwestern part of the country that borders Indonesia. Over the next two years, I learned much that touched me deeply. I traveled quite a bit, as the area I covered was quite large. I spent a lot of time in the villages, teaching how to grow new foods and how to cook them. I also went with the local health workers and helped with immunizations and gave health messages on many different topics. Six months into my stay, I became the director of the agro nutrition project, which included managing several vegetable markets. For the most part, it was work that was rewarding, extremely interesting, and I learned a lot about communication and helping others increase their knowledge of health-based information. I spoke the official language fluently, so I was able to work with many people in remote areas either directly or through a translator.

Many times people would ask me for medical advice or medical help. My knowledge was limited, but I could bandage cuts or wounds, dispense malaria medications, and help with burns or other minor medical needs. On one occasion, while spending a week in a remote Highland village, a mother came up to me with her small infant child. The baby had gotten diarrhea, so she had stopped giving any liquids in the hopes of stopping the flow. This was the local custom. She came to me weeping with her child, asking me to help her. She handed me the child and, as I pulled back the blanket, found that the baby had died. It was extremely dehydrated. There was nothing I could do. I handed the child back to her and explained the situation to her and the reason her baby had died. The people felt badly for the mother but, in the village society, many children crossed over into spirit early from just such circumstances. The next day, we had a town meeting and health talk, and I explained the reason for the child's death and what could be done to help prevent such occurrences from happening again. There were many women that began to change their practices because of my talks and, when the children got diarrhea, they rehydrated instead. Because of that episode, rehydration became one of my most frequent topics in the talks I gave.

I met many people that used local plants as well as shamans. At that time, I was not privy to much of the information, which was well guarded by the practitioners. However, some villagers shared knowledge of the local herbs that I tried, as well as some of the stories of what occurred when they went to visit a traditional healer. At that time, though, I did not put as much stock in some of the local healers as I did with some of the Western medical people working out of the local health jurisdictions. I still was firmly planted within the Western medical model and saw quite a bit of value in it when working with the people.

On one occasion that once again brought me back to the world of spirit, I took a trip to a village called Selbang located in the mountainous northern region. I frequented this village often because there were two other Peace Corps volunteers, and we interacted quite a bit. There was a boy that I had met on one of my early trips named Oscar. He flew out with me on one occasion because he had a broken arm that had not healed correctly. He had to come to Kiunga and have it rebroken. He had no family in town, so I offered him a place to stay with me after his cast was put on. He remained with me several days until he was able to catch a flight back. Oscar was about eleven when I first met him. He had never flown in a plane or ridden in a car before. Many people in the remote villages had never experienced much of the Western amenities that we so often take for granted in the industrialized world. Many others lived even more remotely than those living near the airstrips or waterways, which were the centers of travel for most of Western Province.

During one trip to Selbang, Oscar introduced me to his father. I had never met him on any other occasion, as he was someone who preferred to live in the isolated interior. Oscar stayed in the village, separated from his immediate family, to go to the elementary school situated near the airstrip. Because of the way he would sit all scrunched up into a crouched ball, Oscar's father was a man that appeared smaller than he actually was. However, he was a man that was big among his people. His knowledge of shamanism and working with nature spirits were extensive from real world experience. He considered the remote village of Selbang as civilization, and he seldom came into "town" except to visit with relatives and pick up a few supplies. His eyes were the most remarkable feature about him. They shone extremely bright with an inner fire. He did not speak English or even Tok Pisin, the official language of the country. Oscar translated for me. Oscar's father was a traditional medicine man. I asked him if his father had ever practiced cannibalism. He told me that when he was younger he did, because it was common practice for most people of that area over the age of twenty-five or thirty. I also asked about his spiritual practices. Oscar told me his father talked with the animal spirits around him as well other spirits of the forest. His father believed that all things in the natural world were connected and one. He was happy living away from others. He liked his solitude with his wives, of which he had four. As he spoke, I could not directly understand his words but could feel the innate power that lay within him. His eyes shone brightly and were full of knowledge and power. At that point in time, I wanted to learn more but was not given the opportunity. I still was planted in the world of science and Westernized health, and the question still remained if he would have even been willing to share his knowledge with me. Many of the secrets that these men held were still well guarded. Just meeting him did much to keep the spark alive, knowing there was more to the world than it seemed.

Two years passed quickly. I spent a lot of the time traveling throughout the northern half of the province, honing my public health and public speaking skills in the remote villages. Many were only accessible via boat or small plane. I used many techniques to get various subjects across to the local people. I often felt more like a traveling minstrel show than a teacher, but sometimes those two go hand in hand. I gained a lot of valuable information regarding the disease processes and the use of Western medicine to treat physical maladies. When I wasn't out in the bush, I spent a lot of time at the Kiunga health center. It was a small center with ten beds and an operating room. I was allowed to view more surgeries as I got to know the medical staff. Although the center was remote, the doctors and nurses were well trained by Australian teachers. Through them, I gained a lot of hands-on experience as well as technical knowledge. It was a perfect segue way into the next phase of my life as I returned to the U.S. in October of 1990. I was a different person than when I left, much more mature and well-traveled, and I was married. I met Enny, the woman of my dreams, in Indonesia. Together we came back to Chicago while I was transitioning to the next stage of my life, working with the Quinault Indian Nation in Washington state.

My new wife, Enny, and I drove cross-country to Pacific Beach, Washington, a small town located on the Pacific Ocean. The year 1991 was a year of many changes as I began my new employment as an environmental health specialist. This was much the same job as I had done in South Dakota. The work was preventative in nature. There were many inspections required as well as a lot of community education. I was based out of the public works department. Because of my past experience, within six months I was made public works director. Within eight months, I was offered the opportunity to become an emergency medical technician (EMT) and to join two local volunteer ambulance services. The first was in Taholah, which is the main village of the Quinault Indian Nation, and the second was North Beach Ambulance based out of Pacific Beach. Both services desperately needed volunteers. Training was intense with one hundred twenty hours of instruction and hands-on experience This was a wonderful opportunity for me, because it gave me a lot of first hand experience helping others in life and death emergency situations. It also exposed me more to the death process, which kept me searching more deeply for the meaning and purpose of life.

My intuitiveness was trained and heightened during this period. I was given a pager tied into the 911 emergency system. When volunteers needed to respond to an emergency, a beeping tone first would be sounded followed by verbal instructions giving the location and nature of the call. Soon after receiving my pager, I began to awaken shortly before the pager would go off. The first couple of times I thought it was coincidence, but when I would awaken, I would feel an urgency to get up and start moving. By the third time it happened, I was up and moving when it went off. This became the norm for me. I would wake up in the middle of the night and recognize the sense of urgency. Quickly getting up, I almost would be dressed and out the door before the pager went off. This would put me at the firehouse first. I would have the ambulance out of the garage and warming up before any of the other volunteers would pull up in their cars. They were amazed at the speed at which I was able to respond. I soon got a reputation among the other volunteers for being precognitive. It was an asset because we were able to get to the scene more quickly which helped on many occasions.

In one instance, it helped save an infant's life. On Christmas Day in 1994, we received a call about a woman having a baby in the parking lot of the local store. The store was right next to the fire hall, so all the supplies were nearby. I was already up and moving before the pager went off, so I was on the scene quickly. The woman was in the back seat of her Chevrolet, in labor, and ready to deliver. No sooner had I pulled up and assessed the situation, when the baby's head began to crown. I did not even have time to put on a pair of rubber gloves as the child passed through the vaginal canal and into my hands smoothly and quickly. I barely had time to get into the back seat. The umbilical cord was wrapped around the baby's neck, and he could not breathe. Luckily, at that point, an obstetrics nurse arrived and helped me unwrap the cord. The baby boy quickly began to breathe. I then was given all the supplies I needed to cut the cord, wrap the baby up, and begin administering oxygen. A tragic situation had been averted. The mother healed quickly, and the boy grew up strong and healthy. Each Christmas I remember the mother and child in my thoughts and prayers.

I volunteered for six years and went on more than four hundred calls. I was on call twenty-four hours a day when I was in the area, which was often. I also trained as a firefighter and was sent to the firefighter academy in North Bend, Washington. If a call came in during work hours, I would always respond if I was able. I found that I had an innate knowledge in emergency situations of what to do to help the person in need. Many times quick action was needed to save lives. Other times, the person already had crossed over into spirit by the time we arrived, and there was nothing much we could do for them. Harder still were the times when the person crossed over in transport to the hospital. Because we were so rural, getting from the scene to the hospital often took almost an hour. In extremely critical circumstances, this was too long. It then was up to us to keep the body alive until help that was more able could arrive for resuscitation.

The first time I had to do cardiopulmonary resuscitation was in the hospital. While in the local hospital dropping off a patient, another ambulance service brought in a man in cardiac arrest. I still was fairly new, so I was asked if I wanted experience with the skill. I agreed and began doing chest compressions. This went on until it was decided that the patient was not going to revive after about twenty minutes. Throughout the process, I began to put my psychic senses out. I tried to sense the presence of the person on whom we were working. I attempted to find his spiritual essence in the room. I had read many books on near death experiences, so I was hoping to find evidence of a spiritual nature. I looked above the body and around the room, and I also put my intuitive senses on alert, but I could not discern his presence. I now know that he was present in the room with us throughout the resuscitation attempt. Although at that time I was not able to connect with the man that crossed over to spirit before me, having the openness and desire to try at least was the key to opening myself further to more experiences.

I had many more chances to attempt this as I witnessed death many times in the six years of volunteer work. There also were many success stories. It was those successes that kept me going, but the cost was high. I began to put emotional armor up around myself because of all the hurt and pain I was feeling. I was empathetic, and my being was absorbing the pain and suffering I witnessed at least several times a week. I held a lot of pain within me that I did not know how to release. I was given the opportunity to use hypnotherapy and guided meditation, and it did help quite a bit but not nearly enough. It was this desire to change and heal that started my search again for more alternative methods. It was difficult for me at first to locate someone I could trust. This was due to my immersion at that time into Western medical beliefs. I had begun to lose myself in the world of technology and physicality, as many do that become entrenched in that reality.

In 1995, I transferred from public works and became the community health director based out of the Quinault Indian Nation Clinic. I supervised programs relating to public health nursing, nutrition, diabetes, and other public health functions. I was directly involved in making policy and procedure changes throughout many aspects of the health center. In that capacity, I was given first hand knowledge of how Western medicine worked and the many shortcomings that come with it. This is due to viewing health in a purely physical manner. There have been many wonderful advances in the last fifty years in technology and the understanding of the physical processes of the human body. However, the emotional and spiritual nature of people still eludes many in this field. Too often, they don't see these aspects as relevant. Happily, there is a new awakening of many that are going outside the mainstream viewpoints. This is not only patients, but nurses and doctors as well. This is leading to advances in health care as a whole. However, there still are many issues with Western medicine. One of the biggest I have seen is how complicated it is all becoming. As degenerative diseases are taking over our world, the prolonging of life in such a complex and increasingly specialized system is becoming difficult. Health care itself is being crushed under the burden of regulation and not accepting the potential of death as an outcome.

Westernized society views death as an unacceptable outcome of the hospital experience. Our society has become so litigious and blaming that hospitals and doctors have become afraid to try anything new outside direct technology. The rules imposed by regulatory agencies also discourage such a path. This has led health care down a road that is very fear based and narrow in focus. This system also reflects our society as a whole. Fear of death and loss blocks much of our growth. Happily, the veils that separate the knowledge of death from our physical life are becoming thinner. Those that have crossed over are now more easily able to interact to let us know it is OK, and that physical death is not the end for us but only another part of growth and development. As we lose the fear of death and begin to look deep within ourselves, we will understand that in each of us is the power to good heath and well-being. As we make this discovery, we are better able to live our lives without the fears that we hold as our truths. For many, the search to better health has led them to energy healing. Many Western health care workers also have begun to follow this path. There are many forms available from which to choose. For me, it was Reiki. It helped to remove the emotional armor I had put up, as well as opened the way to a wider view of spirituality, which I had been searching for all those years.

4

Discovering Reiki: Bright Light Shines Through

Reiki is very powerful healing energy. I was introduced to it in the spring of 1998. Reiki is a form of hands-on healing that uses the concept of universal life force energy flowing through all things. It is a belief that has been around since the beginning of time on this planet and practiced in many forms. With regards to using Reiki energies, the practitioner channels this life force energy most commonly through their hands to the object of their attention, i.e., a person, plant, or animal. Each Reiki practitioner has to be attuned by a person that holds the rank and attainment of mastery, although this title varies by school and method taught. The Reiki attunement brings the practitioner into vibrational harmony with the energies so that they can be passed through the body and given to others for healing and enlightenment.

There are three levels of Reiki. The first level primarily concentrates on healing the physical aspects of a person's being. Level two works with the emotional aspects of a person as well as concentrates on distance healing. Level three or the master level includes the ability to pass on this knowledge to others. This is the level attained by teachers. Reiki is passed on not only by book learning, but its prime component is the attunement, which is passed from teacher to student. In this way, each Reiki practitioner is connected to each other.

Reiki is a holistic form of energy healing and is able to work with all aspects of a being, the physical, emotional, and spiritual. Symbols are given at each stage of the learning process. The purpose of these symbols is for increasing the focus of Reiki energies, protection, distance healing, and many other applications. There are only several basic symbols that most Reiki practitioners use but, as time unfolds, other symbols have come forward through different teachers to be used by various branches and schools. The symbols are used before a session, or to create areas of protection from negative energies, or to clear negative energies from a space.

Reiki is a high vibrational form of energy and is intelligent. It will go where it is needed without much conscious direction. It never can be used for harm and is only used for good. Most Reiki practitioners have the belief that this energy comes straight from God and so is of the highest order. Reiki has no religious dogma attached to it, so people of any faith can use it. A man named Dr. Mikao Usui brought it into our recent time period in the late 1800s from Japan. It was gifted to him during years of searching for ancient methods of hands-on healing that came to fruition after a meditation on Mount Kurama-yama. Ms. Hawayo Takata brought it to the U.S. after World War II.

I do not believe there are any "better" or "worse" forms of energy healing. It is all good because it comes from the source of all things. It is just a matter of what each person resonates to and feels comfortable with. In this manner, healing can occur more effectively and efficiently. Reiki has many aspects that I have felt comfortable with since my attunement to level 1 in 1998. The first is that the Reiki practitioner is not the one that should claim he or she heals the client. Each person has the ability to heal himself or herself. Reiki simply gives each person the extra energy to boost the healing potential of the body. Reiki also helps remove any blockages throughout the body that can be caused by emotional or physical trauma and, in some instances, past or present karma. When these blocks are removed, healing takes place more quickly and on a deeper level. Reiki also can be used to heal ourselves, as well as others. Not only are we able to help others heal, but also we can use the same energies for ourselves to remove these same types of blocks.

Secondly, and I think more importantly, Reiki helps to open the innate abilities each of us has hidden within ourselves. The physical healing aspects of Reiki can be a small percentage of what it actually brings to each person. The attunement process energizes and opens a pathway that awakens our spirit. Part of the process is the opening of the Crown and Third Eye chakras at the top of the head and on the forehead between the eyes. These are the centers of our psychic and intuitive abilities. They are the doorways to our own self-awareness. Through increasing our self-awareness and unlocking our true potentials, we are able to access higher realms of consciousness and sentience. Higher intuitive abilities not only allow us to communicate more deeply with our true selves, but also those beings in a higher state of vibrational existence. We are able to access our angels, spirit guides, and loved ones that have crossed over into these realms. The veil between these worlds is thin and can be reached.

Some people like to use the healing potential of Reiki without the dramatic opening. Occasionally, people are not ready to access that deeper knowledge, and they need time to assimilate the energies before they take such a step. Each person is allowed to grow according to his or her needs and desires. Reiki works for the highest good of each individual. What may work wonderfully for one person, another person may take a completely different approach and get the same results. Reiki is energy of individuality; it tailors itself for the best outcomes.

Reiki is energy of highest vibrational quality. Life force energies are all around us. They are like a rainbow with different spectrums of vibration. There is a certain portion that can be used for good, or another that can be used for selfish, darker purposes. There are different schools of thought about Reiki, but I am going to relate my thoughts on the subject through years of experience. The Reiki attunement process allows the practitioner to access those energies of an extremely high vibrational quality. As each practitioner begins the process of bringing life force energies into their being to channel to another recipient, only those in the spectrum where Reiki exists are permitted to enter. All others are filtered out. In this way, these healing energies are transferred from the surrounding abundant energy supply, filtered, and then channeled through to the recipient, who receives those energies. Thus, Reiki always is used to help and can never be used to harm. The extent of this help depends on the openness of the receiver to these energies. A person who brings strong disbelief to a Reiki session can continually and consciously block the energies. At the end of the session, they may feel slightly relaxed but nothing more. They created their own outcome through their inability to relax and let the energies work in the way they were intended.

Reiki sessions can be done for animals, plants, objects, and even multiple people at one time. During a session for a human being, the client (or receiver) typically lies in the prone position on a massage table, although a medical exam table, the floor, or a bed is equally suitable. Reiki energies can be transferred in person anywhere two people can meet-even outside under a tree.

The Reiki practitioner may begin anywhere on the body depending on their training and preference. I like to start at the solar plexus, the point where the cord ties the spiritual to the physical body. I do this to connect to the client on a physical, emotional, and spiritual level. The practitioner then lays their hands on the client wherever they intuitively feel it is needed. There are various methods such as starting at the head and working down to the feet. The practitioner also may concentrate on areas that are more negatively affected. This method often is used in cases of trauma, cancer, severe back pain, and other conditions.

In part because of the individualized qualities of Reiki, each client's experience will be unique. One of the most common physical sensations is a feeling of heat emanating from the practitioner's hands. This occurs from the energy transfer between the practitioner and the client. The client also may experience times when they feel light, have incredible emotional releases, see colors, and, in many cases, get so relaxed they fall asleep. The experiences I have witnessed and felt are many and varied. I also have had many clients have spiritual experiences. During the session, they see or hear departed loved ones, angelic presences, or even float above their bodies. These cases are primarily people that are developed along their spiritual path and are more open to these experiences.

After the session, clients express how good they feel. They are often pain free, relaxed, and in a peaceful and blissful state. In the cases where I have been able to work with people more than once, there have been dramatic improvements in flexibility, reduction in pain, speed in healing traumas and surgeries, and, in some cases, remissions of cancers. One of the reasons I continue to use Reiki not only for family and myself, but also for any that desire to use Reiki as a healing modality is because it works. I have had countless instances of confirmations from clients about how much better they feel and how well they have healed. These confirmations also have come from doctors that are amazed at the speed of healing and the overall improvement of their patients.

Western medicine is beginning to see the value of Reiki. It is being used throughout the world in health centers and hospitals. Its usage and popularity is continuing to grow as the medical communities are realizing not only its value to heal, but also how it can dramatically save money for institutions through speedy recoveries and reduced hospital stays. Many doctors and nurses are discovering Reiki and other forms of hands-on healing and integrating it with their own practices or referring out to various practitioners. Another positive aspect of Reiki is that it doesn't take any specialized equipment. It is always with you. All a practitioner needs to do is hold out their hand and transfer the energies. This low-tech approach to health makes it available at any time and any place, which is desirable, especially in more remote areas of the world.

I first was introduced to these wonderful energies while at an indoor air quality workshop on the Suquamish Reservation, right across Puget Sound from Seattle. It was a tribal environmental health professional related learning experience. As part of the workshop, alternative healing methods were introduced because many people in our society have become chemically sensitized to toxins in our environment. As part of the curriculum, two teachers, Randy and Terri Shaw, introduced Reiki. As Randy explained about Reiki, Terri went around the room and spent about five minutes making contact with people on their shoulders and letting the Reiki energies flow. I was the fifth person she came to. I had on a thick shirt and jacket. As she touched me, heat radiated through both of them, and I could strongly feel the energies being passed to me. The contact was only for a short time, but the results were dramatic. It was as if a light switch had been turned on within me. I had been awakened.

As I returned to the hotel after the workshop, I was amazed at the feeling of tranquility that surrounded me. I equated the feeling to the many times I had spent in sensory deprivation tanks or after long periods of meditation and the similar feeling of tranquility and bliss that was achieved. I relayed my thoughts and feelings to Enny about it and my experiences. She also was interested in what had occurred, and we agreed that in several weeks we would go and visit Randy and Terri at their center, Whispering Knowledge.

Several weeks later, we went to see them and learned much more about Reiki energies. Randy and I soon set up a time for me to learn the skill. Since he had no classes scheduled, he agreed to teach me individually. The previous night before my training and attunement, I awoke in the middle of the night. My whole body was sweating, and my hands felt incredibly hot. I also had a dream about becoming attuned to Reiki. I knew that my body and spirit were ready to take the next step. The following day, we began a one-on-one training session lasting two days into the theory, application, and practice of Reiki. After those two days, I was ready to be attuned. I had an intuitive feeling that this was something that was going to deeply change my life. I also felt that it was an event that I had been waiting for a long time. The process of awakening was at hand.

The attunement was performed in Randy and Terri's bedroom. This was a space that was away from the noise of the house. There were many stones and crystals as well as other power objects that made the space highly energetic and perfect for Reiki attunements. They had gone in before me to energetically cleanse the room and to bring in healing angels, spirit guides, and other high vibrational energies. With this attunement, they were going to dramatically open my Third Eye and Crown chakras, as well as place into my hands and heart the first symbol, Cho-Ku-Rei. Randy and Terri were on either side of me, bringing in balance of male and female energies. I sat in a chair with my back straight. As the attunement was performed, the top of my head began to tingle. Through some yogic breathing, strong energies were transferred from my Crown Chakra all the way to the base of my spine. The feeling was intense. Strong, light-filled energies shot through my head and down my back. There was a blinding flash, and my body vibrated. I could feel the energies throughout my whole being. It was incredible. I was deeply energized. From there, the Cho-Ku-Rei symbol was placed into my hands and heart. Randy and Terri congratulated me with a big hug, and I stepped out of the room.

My whole body was vibrating. I was light-headed, and my hands were alive with energy. It was as if I had just awakened from a long sleep. Powerful energies were coursing up and down my body. I wanted to touch everything that was living and transfer the energies that I now had at my disposal. I was filled with light and energy. I felt the touch of the Creator and the universe upon me. I always had been a spiritual person, but this was something that was exciting and new for me. I could now express my spirituality through touch and healing and not just through thanks. I could bring healing energies to anyone and anything that was willing to receive them. I walked around Randy's house and started transferring the energies to plants, his dogs, and anything else I could find that was alive. I was shining!

Soon after my attunement, I began to use it at work. I talked to the clinic director, and she agreed to start having a Reiki clinic twice a month. Randy and Terri started coming out with two tables, and we worked on clients that made appointments. The first clinic we had became full. Others in the community were already familiar with Reiki. The word spread fast. Many of the office workers wanted to try it because of stress. Soon we were working on twelve people in a day. The responses were extremely favorable. The clinics lasted for a year and a half before budget constraints forced us to curtail our activities. We had established a good track record, and many people would come to me during lunch and other certain work hours. Reiki continued to be an alternative and a complement to the care they were receiving through the clinic. In this way, I was able to get a lot of hands-on experience with many people and situations. By the time the clinics were cancelled, I had received my master level attunement and had worked on hundreds of people, giving me great insight into the wonders of Reiki and the unlimited potential within each one of us on this planet. Although the clinics only lasted a year and a half, I was thankful for the time and experience that I received, and because I was able to give back to the communities in which I lived and worked.

Enny and I also used it quite a bit at home. A dramatic usage of Reiki came with the birth of our two daughters. In 1996, Enny had become pregnant with our first daughter, Luna, and developed toxemia. Her whole body became swollen with toxins from the pregnancy. She ended up needing an emergency cesarean to remove Luna before serious complications manifested. After the birth, Enny's kidneys shut down, and she was in a dangerous situation. Her blood pressure remained high and, throughout the process, one of her retinas became detached. She was almost blind in one eye. Her healing was slow and painful, but eventually she returned to good health, including her vision.

In 2000, our second daughter, Mesa, was born. Throughout the pregnancy, Enny received a lot of Reiki from myself and various other friends. Her pregnancy completed with no complications and in relative comfort. Mesa also was born via cesarean, but Enny's recovery was complete and speedy. It occurred so quickly; the doctors and nurses were amazed. She was ready to go home in half the time of the last pregnancy. Her surgery site healed very rapidly. After a week of returning from the hospital, a home health nurse visited us. She also was amazed at the speed of the recovery of the surgery site and had come expecting complications because of the past pregnancy. Enny was up and healed within a very short period of time. The differences in the experiences with and without the addition of Reiki were dramatic.

My spiritual growth truly began once I received my Reiki 1 attunement. Within a couple more months, I had received my Reiki 2 attunement. On January 19, 1999, I received my Reiki master attunement. It was an event I will not forget. It was incredibly powerful not only because of the change in my own energetic vibration, but also for the events that transpired that day.

I arrived at Randy's in the late morning. It had been raining steadily for several days, as is the norm in the Northwest. I had deeply meditated to be prepared for the changes I knew would occur within me. I was ready. Randy brought me into his room, and we began to go into a deep, guided meditation. I followed his words with my sense of hearing, but also with my spirit. I soon was out of my body, astral traveling. Accompanying me on this journey was a Native American Indian man whom I recently had discovered was one of my main spirit guides. We joined hands and began to rise out of the room. I saw myself sitting in the chair with Randy beside me. I proceeded out through the ceiling of the house and up into the sky. I traveled higher and higher, out into space, and above the earth. I saw the earth below me, a blue-and-white ball. It became smaller and smaller as I whisked through the cosmos.

Soon I was in a room filled with a bright white light. I was unsure where and how this room existed. I knew I was no longer in my body, so I was in a more energetic form and corresponding environment. In this room were many other masters. Collectively, they held vast amounts of knowledge. There were at least a couple hundred of them. Their white and multicolored robes shimmered and shifted their hues. A feeling of incredible love washed over me. A congratulatory feel hummed throughout the space as they welcomed me to their corner of the universe. From among their ranks came one that shone more brightly. In his hands, he held a shining white orb, radiating incredible energy. He handed that orb to me, and I was instructed to place it into my heart. Taking the orb in my two hands, I did as he instructed. A powerful feeling of love, power, and strength came over me. I was awash in pure God-centered light. The feeling is something that I cannot describe with simple words. I felt extremely empowered. Much too soon, the energies subsided. The one that had given me the orb embraced me. I felt a deep feeling of congratulations and heard "Welcome" that was spoken not with a physical sense of hearing but of mental understanding. The rest of the light-centered beings also closed in towards me and surrounded me with even more love and congratulations. The feeling of all that love was once again inde-scribable. After a few moments, they stepped back and cleared a space around me. It was time for me to return to earth to continue my work. I was drawn out of the light-filled room and back into the void of space with many stars all around me. I held the hand of my spirit guide, and we sped through the cosmos until we reached earth again. It became larger and larger until I soon was back into the room and my body.

I returned from my experience filled with joy. I was awestruck as to the impli-cations of the journey I just had taken. It took several minutes to get my bearings and my earth legs again, but I soon was somewhat grounded and able to tell Randy what had transpired. From Randy's end, he watched me as I had made the transition. Around me, he had perceived many of my guides, as well as a lot of shifting and moving energies. As I returned from the journey, he also noticed a remarkable positive change in my overall energy field. Half of my attunement had been completed, and there still was another half to go.

We needed some water, so we took a fifteen-minute break. It still was raining steadily, and the rest of the attunement process was to be done outside in an area that was reserved for highly energetic activities. The area was unprotected, so we were going to get wet. Aloud I respectfully asked the clouds if they would grant us some time to do the attunement without the benefit of getting soaked. After about ten minutes, the rain suddenly abated. Randy and I looked at each other, slightly surprised that our request had been answered so easily, and said, "Let's go."

We walked several minutes to the spot and got mentally and energetically pre-pared. As we came to the attunement space, approximately twenty ravens flew into the trees around us and began to caw noisily, announcing their presence. It was another great sign. In Northwest American Indian lore, the raven is a symbol of knowledge and enlightenment. The raven is a teacher, imparting wisdom and bringing it from darkness to light. The raven also is a vocalizer, helping to teach the speech of nature and other animals.

As the attunement began, the clouds ceremoniously parted, and the sun shone down directly upon us in the exact spot we were sitting. The sunshine hit us and warmed upon our faces. As Randy completed the ritual and the master attunement, I again felt the incredible and familiar energies wash over me. Once again, I was buzzing. When the attunement was finished, the clouds covered the sky, the sun disappeared, and the ravens flew away. We walked back to the house, and a gentle rain began again. I graciously thanked all that had helped me with my transition as I took another step deeper into the light of the Creator.

How and why did all of these seemingly fantastic events occur? Did forces unseen and unknown control the weather? How did the ravens know to come to that spot at that time? It all relates to connectedness and working with energies of the highest light. All is possible on this planet. It is only ourselves that limit what can occur for us. Randy and I were open and aware that anything could happen. We both understood as these things were occurring that high vibrational energies were at work and were there to help impart them to us during the attunement process. I was not simply Keith anymore but reclaimed my place as a master. This is not an egoistic state of mind, but a reawakening of what was already there. This can be true for anyone on this planet. We are all masters with the same capabilities and power, just as it was for me that day. The universe is available to bring the same energy and awakening for anyone that searches. How quickly we are able to learn and assimilate this is up to each one of us. I have moved forward quickly because I have not had fear or let fear stop me. I also question, but at the same time accept, knowing it is from the Creator and all is possible.

My Reiki attunements were fairly dramatic. Some people have similar experiences, and for others it is subtle. Often it is more of a gradual unfolding of the energies and abilities. It can take a few days to several weeks for most people to fully feel the changes that have occurred from the attunement. One of the most frequent comments I get right after giving an attunement is a feeling of tingling in the hands and top of the head. They also may feel ungrounded or spacey. This is due to the opening of the Crown Chakra at the top of the head. One of the main purposes of the attunement is to fully open the Crown Chakra so that the individual can channel a larger amount of energy.

There are physical changes that take place as well. Normally, a detoxification process occurs. The body purges itself of many of the physical and emotional toxins that may be present. This can create emotional releases, such as crying for no apparent reason, slight flu-like symptoms and fever, extremely lucid dreams and deep sleep, diarrhea, and mild withdrawals from substances such as caffeine and alcohol. This is the high vibrational energies entering to bring balance to the body. Emotional and chemical pollutants are purged, leaving a feeling of "lightness of being." It is a good chance to get a fresh start with our bodies and minds if we change our self-destructive behaviors, such as eating junk food, drinking lots of coffee, or eating too many sweets. On the emotional side, it is a chance for us to begin to remove our fears and anxieties and leave the past hurts and guilt behind us. It takes longer for some than others, but doors are opened so that this may occur in a more enlightened state.

Reiki attunements always are interesting. During the attunement process, loved ones, spirit guides, angels, and other beings step forward or are present. The attunement is an awakening for the recipient that is viewed in the realms beyond ours as a time for celebration. Thus, they are there to help add their energies to the event or to celebrate the momentous occasion. During the attunement, loved ones always have stepped forward. I stay attentive and open for those that want to give their congratulations or let the Reiki initiates know they are present. Parents, grandparents, aunts, uncles, and many others come to share the experience. The results are a more energetic atmosphere. To me, this is proof that all of our loved ones stay connected to us even after they have crossed over. They continue to be involved in our lives to help in ways we are not always aware.

Another incredible aspect of Reiki is that it can be sent over distances. Actual physical touch is not a prerequisite for the energies to be sent and received. Time and space are not a limitation. Thus, a person could be in his or her own home performing a Reiki session on someone that is in New York, Hong Kong, or Paris. They would get the full benefit of the energies without the practitioner even being there. For some people, this type of activity may be hard to understand, so I will explain briefly the concepts behind distance Reiki and distance healing.

Each one of us is a transmitter of thoughts and energies. Just as cell phones and satellites transmit signals, so do we as living beings. Our intentions and thoughts are more powerful than most people imagine. Because we cannot see them does not mean they do not exist in some measurable form. Reiki energies are the same. The transmitter is the Reiki practitioner, the receiver the client. When the Reiki practitioner sends the energies through intention to the recipient, they travel over whatever physical distance is needed and connect with the intended recipient. This connection exists on a higher, energetic plane. It is not only a meeting of physical bodies but also of spiritual minds. Reiki is considered a spiritual type of energy and healing because of this deeper link. There are no limitations to its usage and power to do good things. It is pure light-centered and spiritually guided energy. I have found this to be an effective way of reaching many people that otherwise would not have been touched or had the opportunities to heal. With this type of healing, enlightenment also occurs. Some circles consider this type of energy work and healing akin to a miracle. Reiki or other forms of healing energy are no less a miracle than if a person took a computer back to a village in seventeenth century America. To them it would be considered something that is unfathomable. However, to our perceptions and understanding, it is energy and science. Much of what is occurring in the fields of spiritual healing and psychic awareness is beginning to be understood in the ways of science and energy. Once these concepts are understood with more scientific reasoning and less misconception of magic and miracles, the more they will be accepted and used in ways that we can only imagine at this time in our development. I believe many methods that are currently used in Western medicine will be seen within the next two decades as primitive and barbaric. The softer and more energetic methods that work with the body's own healing abilities will be used, limiting therapies tied to radiation, surgery, and pharmaceuticals.

Through Moonglow, I proceeded to offer these services. I wanted to spread the knowledge of the effectiveness of such practices, as well as aid others that were in need. I discovered many people in the world that Western medicine could no longer help and who were looking for alternative therapies for healing. Many of these people were monetarily destitute because the costs associated with Western treatments had left them with no savings and deeply in debt. The services I had to offer were inexpensive and often times free to those in dire need. It was a good arrangement as I was just beginning my practice and was able to improve my abilities quickly without the pressures of high expectations. The results of the work that I performed on a regular basis began to amaze even me. The constant positive feedback I received, and the stories of healing and life-changing results touched my heart each time. Distance sessions became an integral part of my week. On average, I was doing thirty to forty distance sessions per month with regular clients that would work with me frequently. Many of the people I encountered did some remarkable healing that surprised not only them, but also their doctors and families. Word of mouth kept me quite busy.

There were some amazing transformations on my end as well. My intuitive abilities really began to blossom and grow as I spent hours connecting with people on many different levels. I became an adept medical intuitive. Within moments of connecting to a person or animal, I could tell all the major areas that needed the healing energies. This also occurred with people I would meet in person. Just by spending several moments with someone, I could tell where they were having blocks in the body or areas that were causing them pain. Sometimes I would mention this to them, and they would look at me with surprise, wondering how I had such knowledge. I could see their ailments. Once I began the distance sessions, I would proceed to concentrate on those areas as well as intuitively listen to any other messages for that person. Their origin may have been due to emotional or spiritual needs. Often not only the physical issues of the person would become known to me, but also the blocks from emotional traumas that had occurred that needed to be cleared. Releasing emotional issues and clearing blocks aids in the healing of physical ailments and symptoms. True recovery from all ailments, those of the physical body and the emotional body, will occur.

After the sessions, I would get feedback about how clients were doing and the dramatic stories of their experiences during or after the sessions. I want to share some of them to give a better idea of what had occurred. Most of the time, the only information I initially would receive before the session would be their name and a time and date to connect. At the appointed time, they were encouraged to lie down and relax, put on soft music and subdued lighting, and light a candle or two. After the session, I would write what I found and concentrated on.

In this first account, Mavis was having problems throughout her body, especially in her neck, back, and shoulders, as well as reproductive area and knees. After writing to Mavis and relaying the information I received, this was her reply:

"Hi Keith,

I found it easy to relax and felt wrapped in a warm, gentle energy with presence. I felt the pain in the neck subside a lot. I have much more flexibility this morning. I also felt surges of expansion and contraction in the third eye. Interior lights, memories arising, and part of me just said, 'Peace, peace, peace.'

You picked up on the female problem, which I don't remember mentioning. There were several times I felt a new intensity of being wrapped in the Reiki. And I felt renewal. I slept well.

Thank you, this is deeply appreciated!"

I worked with Mavis several more times, and most of her health issues healed completely. She no longer needed my services. This was the goal I consistently try to achieve. It became common that those working together with me would heal quite well and in a relatively short period of time.

Many distance sessions are much more dynamic than just healing on a physical or emotional level. It also can transcend into other planes. With this next example, information about her past life came through. Her name was Isabelle. She had various issues throughout her body that needed healing. She did not give me any foreknowledge of her conditions. She asked if I also could work on past life information for her. This session was one of the first ones that I did where the Reiki was coupled with the past life information. After writing to her about what I found physically during the session, I then wrote about her past life.

I wrote:

"The main view that I saw was of a man (which would have been you) in a lush green tropical forest. I got a strong message it was South America. You were a rainforest native. You had a grass house, many family members around. No one was wearing much clothing. It was like you would see on National Geographic. I felt a piercing blow to the neck, which would have ended your life. It was as if you fell on a sharp object that punctured the carotid artery. So, you were a South American man, living a traditional rainforest hunter/gatherer lifestyle."

Her reply was:

"Keith, some absolutely amazing things happened to me during the session. First, you are right on the money about my left knee—complete tear of the ACL in yoga class, of all things, that was two years ago, but we still have ups/downs with it. Ironically, I started having hip pain (left hip) several months ago, with no injury or problem, just hurts. The doctor attributes most of this to a birth defect that affects my bottom vertebrae, right side, which causes me a great deal of pain regularly, especially in the reproductive areas. So, great call!

Ok, for the amazing part, I'm lying on the couch, and about 11:10 I get a hot tingling sensation on the top of my head, after awhile it moved to my hip, then my knee. It felt really good!!! Then, out of nowhere, I got propelled off the couch, on to the floor with an intense pain in my lower back, and then it was gone. I made enough noise to wake my husband, so he came out to check on me—was quite amused by the whole thing. My back is feeling GREAT, thank you much! Better than what several doctors and chiropractors have been able to do over the last 15 years!

Funny you should mention a South American connection. I was in Cancun about twelve years ago and did all the tourist stuff, including a trip to Chichen Itza. I started to climb the pyramid, and I became deathly sick, like throwing up, bor-

dering on passing out. I turned chalk white, heard a "whirring" noise, and started shaking. I had to lie down on the steps until some nice man on his honeymoon helped me back down. I was only 20 feet up! My mother was with me, and she couldn't believe her eyes. She said it was like I had seen a ghost. Once I got back down on the ground, I was fine. The color came back in my face, no sweating, and not queasy. She's always teased me about that because the next day, we went to another pyramid, and I went right up it like it was nothing.

Thank you so much for "fixing my back," and thank you for a wonderful experience. Now, perhaps I'll sleep through the night!

Light and love,

Isabelle"

I believe that at the moment she began to climb the pyramid, something triggered her past life memories, and they began to come into her conscious mind. It was something that she did not know how to deal with at the time, so she shut it all out and became sick. This is not an uncommon reaction when something we cannot quite decipher happens to us. Sometimes these issues are so deeply locked away to the conscious mind, that when they begin to come to the forefront, the mind shuts down also affecting the physical body.

The physical movement of her entire body, the propelling off the couch, was quite interesting. This type of occurrence has happened to several clients during sessions. It is most often associated with back issues. I believe that the unexpected movements help to bring the back into alignment. It seems very unorthodox but, in all cases, it has been successful. Isabelle's was the only case that I worked on that someone actually was moved to that extent. There have been others that have sat up suddenly or felt a gentle push underneath them. Having actual movement of this type during Reiki is quite rare but, for this client, effective.

This next client needed not only healing for the physical aspects of his well-being, but also for the emotional disharmony that spread throughout his being. Allen had never had a distance Reiki session before. After I was finished, I wrote him and told him all that I had found. There were some clear messages that came through about expressing himself as well as his relationship with his parents. He replied:

"Hi Keith!

Well, that was a beautiful experience! I certainly felt the Reiki session on my end for sure. At times it was noticeable, then other times it was subtle. I could feel the energy move to different areas of my body. At one point, I surprised myself as I drifted off to deep relaxation by releasing a short little laugh.

I do catch myself holding my jaw tightly. I also have been told I grind my teeth at night on rare occasions (or rarely do I get caught). Coincidently, I just went to the dentist today also. I think you are right about the solar plexus and abdominal area. I have been more out of balance emotionally as of late....Now as far as the legs are concerned, you totally nailed it. My right leg and ankle were broken. In fact, I still have and will have two titanium screws in my ankle. I broke it during a bouldering mishap a little over two years ago. Wow. Is that the Twilight Zone music I hear?

I have been struggling with how to express myself as an artist for nearly all my life. It has reached a point of being nearly unbearable in the last year and a half. I know that discipline is what I need, and then the ideas will flow and the methods will become clearer.

The answers all ring true, and I will need some time for me to absorb and appreciate them fully. The message you gave me to connect with my father was especially powerful. I have a superficial relationship with him. The skeptic (he's always there) is impressed that you nailed the relationships (or lack of) with both my father and mother. I could have been orphaned or they could be long dead.

I very much wish to express my gratitude to both you and Enny for sharing your talents. You have given me quite a bit to think on. So thank you.

Namaste!

Allen"

Often the clients with whom I work feel intense energies. These are the Reiki energies working to remove blocks in the body, thus allowing the healing energies to flow more freely. In this next instance, John felt those energy blocks break free. I relayed to him that he was dealing with stress issues, as well as clenching his jaw. In this case, John almost began to astral travel. This was something he had been trying to accomplish and, in the relaxed state that occurred, he was almost able to accomplish it.

He wrote:

"Thanks for the great session. I had trouble relaxing and connecting for a bit, but then it happened. Two distinct things—toward the end I literally felt a blockage clear. I was suddenly much lighter and freer than I'd felt in a while. I also felt three distinct taps on my left shoulder, which shook me out of my meditative state at the end of the session. I thought that was interesting. I started to leave my body once or twice but snapped back before it happened. I'm still working on that one, no luck yet.

During the session, there was intense heat around my neck and on the front of my face. This stayed with me most of the time until the energy block broke, and then it was gone.

I do computer work all day and then come home and jump on the computer again. I also read as much as I can, so the stress energies are certainly justified. I also catch myself clenching my jaw a lot and have been trying to break this one lately.

Thanks again for the session. I have been more relaxed and in tune today, and I can almost feel myself continuing to open up."

Many times the Reiki energies will leave a person feeling relaxed, yet energized. This is deep balancing going on throughout the body. There are hundreds more documented stories that I could relay, but I think the point has been made. Reiki works! It works on so many levels. I also believe this to be the case with many other forms of healing energies not just Reiki. Accessing higher healing energies can create such powerful changes in a person's life. The more we are aware of the potential that is within each of us, the easier it is to tap into that potential for health, overall balance, and the awakening of the spirit within us.

5

Who Is That Looking over My Shoulder? Oh, It's My Spirit Guide!

Reiki immediately opened the door for me to connect with my spirit guides. Connecting to our spirit guides is an important step in our growth. Spirit guides are constantly with us throughout our lives even though we may not be aware of them. They are exactly what the name implies. They are people/animals/beings that are in a higher plane of existence. They are here to help guide us through our life on this planet for the time we are here. They are not here to harm us and have nothing but pure loving intentions for our success and happiness.

Spirit guides are one of the first types of spiritual energies that a person can connect to once they have consciously chosen to be open to the experience. One misconception is that we are the recipients of their attentions. The fact is that most of the time we choose our own spirit guides to help us fulfill goals that were determined by our higher or spiritual self before we returned in our present form. That higher or spiritual self knows our purpose in this lifetime, even if we are consciously unaware of it.

Interaction between our higher self and our spirit guides is constant. Once a person is aware of their spirit guides, they can interact with them in their waking hours. Some guides are with us most of our lives. Others come and go as needed. It is like a revolving door with guides, angels, loved ones, and others, coming in and out of our life as the situation warrants.

Spirit guides may be here to help teach us a skill or to help fuel an interest that may blossom into a life's work. They may be present to protect us from danger or to help cushion the impact of falls, accidents, etc. They may be with us to relay messages. Many kinds of spirit guides are with us always. We are never alone and always are looked after, even if we do not perceive their presence. Our lives are constantly monitored but not with judgment. Our guides exist in a higher state of being that is above the negative state of having to judge others. They accept the circumstances and attempt to help us attain higher consciousness. They are here to guide us, not admonish us. Many of them have been through the same circumstances we have, which is why they are chosen by us to be with us. We should not feel self-conscious about them being around us once we learn of their presence. They already know us well and are not shocked or surprised by anything we do. Their job is to help us become the best we can be. It is a constant journey that will take many lifetimes, and that is understood by all.

The spirit guides we have with us also may be chosen by others and help many people at once. This is possible because there are no limits to time, space, and form in the higher spiritual dimensions. Mahatma Gandhi had millions of followers and, to this day, millions still look to him for guidance. Had he been limited to one form, this would not have been possible. There are no limitations for those in a more highly evolved spiritual state. Ghandi achieved omnipresence, as do many beings that ascend to higher realms of vibration. This higher realm of vibration is available to all within the universe, but one must work toward that state. Jesus, Buddha, Mohammed, and Krishna exist in millions of places at one time, attending to those in need of their love and healing powers and listening to their lamentations.

The spirit guides that we have with us also have spirit guides with them. As our guides are above us in experience and awareness, their guides are as well. Above those spirit guides exist spirit guides. It is a multifaceted layer upon layer of knowledge and beings that are all working together to help one another achieve ultimate enlightenment. Thus, all beings are constantly striving for growth through many lifetimes and many different experiences. Becoming a more highly evolved being is what helping as a spirit guide is about. Growth never stops for any soul. It is a constant learning and growing experience. Giving of ourselves through loving, unselfish acts is part of that growth process. Those that choose to be guides also are helping in their own spiritual growth. As they help to guide us, they also learn many things in the process. It is all intertwined. After we cross over into spirit, there is a good chance that we will be a spirit guide for others. In this way, we grow and learn, with the ultimate goal being higher ascension so that we will not have to continue to reincarnate into this third dimensional form. How long this takes depends on each person's spiritual growth and the rate at which each person achieves this. Being a spirit guide for others helps in this ascension process.

I began working with my guides in 1998, the day before I received my Reiki 1 attunement. Randy Shaw gave me a guided meditation tape he had put together.

It was a scenario in which the listener would connect with his or her spirit guides and meet them. The evening before my Reiki attunement, I decided to try it, because I was eager to discover the results.

I lied down, so that I could get comfortable and relaxed. I turned the tape on and began to follow the instructions to get myself into a deeply relaxed state of mind. Soon I was ready to meet my guides. At one point in the scenario, I was to walk down a path to a doorway. Behind that doorway was a room that had my spirit guides waiting to meet me. With excitement, I mentally opened the door and walked in. It was empty. At first, I thought maybe I wasn't ready or I needed several more attempts to achieve the desired results. Then suddenly, standing before me was Rod Serling. As a point of reference, he was the host and main writer for the TV shows Twilight Zone and Night Gallery. I stood there and looked at him, thinking, "What the heck is this? Rod Serling is my spirit guide?" He then held out his hand for me to shake it. He had a large grin on his face. It was one of happiness, but also one of mirth. I shook his hand. He silently looked at me with that quirky smile of his as if to say, "Welcome to the Twilight Zone." Then he promptly disappeared. I roused myself from the meditation and figured the whole experience was something I made up in my head. It was a letdown because I was really hoping something would happen for me that evening. I figured the next day I could try it again and see what would happen.

The following day I received my Reiki 1 attunement. That night I decided to try again to contact my spirit guides. They came through almost immediately after I was relaxed. I suddenly was overtaken by a powerful presence. Green, smoky energies danced behind my eyes and brightened. I knew then that this was not my imagination. My heart rate increased and adrenaline coursed through my body. The greenish energies became faces pushing through the smoke. One, then another would appear, then fade. They were all different. Some were men. Some were women. More than ten revealed themselves to me that night. Several minutes elapsed, and the green smoky energy dissipated. The intense energies that had engulfed me subsided. Everything slowed down, and my perceptions returned to my immediate surroundings. I sat bolt upright. With my heart still racing, I thought to myself, "I have connected to spirits! They do exist!"

Nothing like that had ever happened to me before. I believed my experiences were valid and not just something I had made up due to expectations. They were present not only visually, but also on a deeper level that was difficult to pinpoint. I had felt their presence intuitively. It also had become clear that the night before, when I encountered Rod Serling, it was indeed him and he was saying, "Welcome to the Twilight Zone!"

Everything changed quickly after that evening. Initially, I was a little frightened after the experience. My equilibrium was thrown off. However, it quickly returned, and I was excited to explore my new knowledge to the fullest. The next evening I replicated the same conditions. Once again, sentient energy engulfed me, and there was dancing, smoky energies moving behind my eyes. This time I relaxed and let it all flow. In the swirling energies, I once again saw the outlines of faces. After several moments everything subsided. I was hoping for a deeper connection and more information, but the encounter once again was brief. I felt energized and excited. I was off to a great start. After the second encounter, the knowledge of their existence was more deeply ingrained within me. A very important door had been opened, and I was determined to discover much more about those that chose to help me through my life. I knew the experiences I had were but a glimpse of a much greater reality. It was just a matter of time before I gained a better understanding of my guides and my abilities to help others discover theirs.

For a few months, I interacted with my spirit guides in a similar fashion. I would connect to them through meditation. I continued to experience them as different colored energies and not as more fully formed and recognizable people, animals, or beings. They came to me as different colored energies, and I soon realized the colors had meaning. For example, when I encountered the green energies, it related to the guides there to help me with healing. Pink was family members or loved ones. White was higher vibrational guides, such as angels, and purple was teacher guides.

Spirit guides can offer much that is not available in the physical world. They are able to give us knowledge and teaching through intuitive experience. Teacher guides are here to help us with our desires to learn and to teach or re-teach us knowledge that has been lost through the transition from spiritual to physical world. There have been many times that my guides have come in to teach me subjects that I asked about or had a need to learn. Knowledge is plentiful throughout the universe. As physical beings, we are accustomed to going to a teacher, paying a compensatory fee for their services, and learning from them slowly, absorbing the knowledge through speech and action. However, learning from guides is much quicker, and the knowledge learned is much more deeply ingrained.

One example of this was when I was beginning to learn to meditate. At Moonglow, I had erected a tepee to reflect, do some basic meditation, or tune in for spiritual messages. However, I desired a more structured approach to my meditation, because it always had been difficult for me to quiet my mind. I put two empty chairs in front of me and asked the universe for help and guidance. Within several minutes, two Chinese men dressed in long flowing robes sat before me. One wore red, one blue. I realized they were starting with the concepts of yin and yang, with the red being the energetic, blood-flowing meditation, and the blue being the cooling, calm type of meditation. Over several days, they taught me different breathing techniques and instilled in me knowledge to help quiet my mind. I augmented this knowledge with physical aids, such as books and CDs, but the time spent with the two teacher guides sped my learning up dramatically.

The learning was accomplished through visualizations and intuitive experience. During the breathing lessons, I could feel within my body what to do. It was not so conscious as it was innate. I felt deep within my lungs and diaphragm the correct way to breathe. When I tried it, it was natural and fit perfectly. The visualizations and lessons on learning how to sit, focus my mind, and center myself also were imparted through telepathic means. It was unlike a Hollywood movie where the men would appear as semisolid beings, talking to me as a physical teacher would. The visual part was through my psychic centers, or third eye, and the speech was not so much individual words but a series of visual messages. During times of meditation, I now will hear comments such as "sit up straight" or "put your feet flat on the floor" if my posture is not correct or I am sitting with legs overlapping or crisscrossed.

Our guides will help us assimilate any type of information that we desire. Being open to the experience and knowledge is all that is needed. If a person has a desire to paint, tuning into your guides or asking a guide that was a painter or has painting knowledge to help will speed the learning process. A physical teacher still may be needed to get the basics down, and practice is necessary, but guides will help make it all happen more smoothly. It also is important to remember that each of us is an important being in the universe, no more or less than anyone that is famous. Painters such as Renoir, Matisse, Van Gogh, or Michelangelo can be called upon to help. They will come to assist in some manner or another to the best of their ability. Asking is all that is required, and help will arrive that is compatible with the need.

Another good example of receiving help happened in 1999 while Enny and I were looking for property to purchase to create our dream of opening Moonglow. We had been looking for about a year to no avail. We tried the Realtors and, many unsuitable investigations later, there still was nowhere we truly felt was a place for us. One day I received an intuitive message to travel up a road I had never been on before. I spotted a hand painted sign nailed to a tree advertising property for sale. As I pulled into the five-acre parcel, I was impressed with the surrounding landscape. There were a couple of issues that I immediately recognized as being potential hardships. It just had been logged except for about an acre and a half, and it would take a lot of time and extra money to develop the property. I also saw that the soil was rocky. Above all that, it was an hour and a half commute from my job working with the Quinaults. I would have to travel from one side of the county to the other. However, I was instantly in love with it. There was a beautiful view of the Olympic Mountains to the north, and foothills and trees surrounded us. There was a state park with a river less than half a mile a way. The energy of the whole area was wonderful. I continually got a strong message from all of our guides that this was the place for us to be and that we needed to purchase it.

I spent some time walking the property line and discovering all that was available in those five acres. The message kept coming through; this was the place for us. Later, after we had finished the initial work building the house, Enny and I discovered that the property was part of our life's path. For much of our lives, we were to constantly work from the basics and build upward. In this way, we would learn much of what we needed to know so that we could relate to and teach others. The property where Moonglow was founded was an extremely difficult property on which to live. There were many rocks in the soil. The ridge we lived on was comprised of glacial till. The ice had melted during the last ice age and dumped its rocky loads throughout the valleys surrounding us. To plant anything, I had to use an iron bar and shovel to shape a small hole. Planting a garden was a major undertaking. Tillers didn't work, and I couldn't use a lawn mower for a long time due to the potential damage the rocks would cause to the rotors and engine. Each spring the rocks appeared on the property as if by magic. It was a completely undeveloped piece of property so everything was done from scratch. Monetarily, we were limited, so much of it had to be done by hand or the occasional loaned tractor or hired bulldozer. It always was hard, back-breaking work. However, throughout it all, I stayed in good shape physically and, when things were completed, the rewards and feeling of accomplishment were terrific. We let the east and west sides of the property grow back naturally, and soon we had a great array of beautiful, natural plants. In the spring and early summer, we had thousands of wildflowers that would grow. From them we created our own flower essences. Wildlife, such as woodpeckers, hawks, deer, coyotes, and many other beautiful animals, found a place to stay and were welcomed. Berries grew back, such as wild blackberries, huckleberries, and salal berries. The extra time that it took me to drive to work, I either listened to books on tape or worked on my intuitive development. With this extra time, I learned many new ideas, as well as had time to develop more deeply many of my blossoming talents. As everything began to take shape, we had a beautiful and tranquil place to live. The rewards from our hard work were truly great.

Spirit guides also can be great protectors. They help keep us out of danger through intuitive messages. Many are the stories of people that get an uneasy feeling before they get on a plane, get into a car, or undertake a journey. Sometimes they have the feeling so strongly that they cancel their flight or the trip itself later to discover that the plane had crashed or some other event occurred that would have endangered their life or caused physical harm. There are other situations that are created by our guides, such as short delays, that keep us out of the wrong place at the wrong time. We get frustrated over minor delays that make us late in some way, but because we missed the event, we may never know what serious accident or injury we avoided. Whenever minor occurrences delay me, I see them as possibly my guides helping to keep me out of danger, thus I do not get frustrated or angry, I just go with the flow.

I had an instance when I was given a strong message that saved my life. One day in 1995, I was on my way home from visiting friends in the nearby town of Aberdeen, Washington. Before I left to go home, I stopped at a local convenience store that I occasionally frequented to pick up some drinks and snacks for the ride home. I usually parked right in front of the store next to the major lane of traffic. This day I got a strong message to park on the side street adjacent to the building. I went inside, finished my shopping, and came out of the building. Just as I walked the several feet from the door to the side of the building, I heard a crash. As I turned around, out of the corner of my eye I could see a huge object fly by that seemed like a rocket. As I turned and focused, a car sped past me on the sidewalk, missing me by about two feet. It continued to career down the sidewalk, jumped the curb on the next street, slammed into a fire hydrant, and finally came to a rolling stop in the yard of a house about two hundred feet from where I stood. The man in the car got out, quite shaken and surprised at where he was. Apparently, he had fallen asleep at the wheel, jumped the curb, drove down the sidewalk until he slammed into the fire hydrant, and came to a stop. Incredibly no people, buildings, or cars had been hit. If I had parked in the front of the building, as I came out of the store and walked to my car I assuredly would have been hit by the vehicle. My guides protected my physical body by guiding me to park on the side of the building instead of the front.

There are many ways each person can connect to his or her guides. Success often depends on how open the person is rather than the technique used. Fear is the single largest barrier to spiritual communication. Fear puts up a big wall that is hard to penetrate. It is important to know that the contact may be something that will shake a person's world, but it is nothing that is going to harm. No being is instantly going to takeover the body of another. Spirit guides will attempt to make the connection gently so that fear and anxiety is kept to a minimum, thus facilitating contact. They want to make the connection. Attempting contact is a big step towards karmic and spiritual growth. They may connect in dreams or in the half-awake, half-asleep state. This is a receptive time when a person is already halfway in the astral realms but also able to remember and know that it is not a dream. Meditation also is a good way for contact. It is important to quiet the mind to be able to hear or see the information as it is given. The information is not auditory or visual in a third dimensional way but more in the mind's eye. Some pictures of people and places or faces may come, or a thought may occur that does not originate from the person's own mind. The presence of another person or people in the room also may be felt. Guided meditation CDs are another way the spiritual connection can be made. The suggestive words and relaxing music quickly can get the mind in a receptive state. Holding or using stones or crystals will enhance the connection. Amethyst, clear Quartz Crystal, Prehnite, or a host of other geological treasures can open the upper chakras so the connection can be facilitated.

Children are very open to their guides and angels. Our daughters, Luna and Mesa, have been interacting since they were very young with their guides and family members who have crossed over into spirit. This is the case with most children. They are very open to spiritual experiences. The world is still new and exciting, and everything is possible. Their chakras are very open and able to receive visitations and interactions by those in the spiritual realms. When children are playing with their "imaginary playmates," they are often spiritual visitors. To the children, they are just as real as those in physical form.

I am going to share a few stories that relate to our two children and their interaction with family members that have crossed over or spiritual playmates. The first concerns a mini van that we purchased. It was a reduction special on the lot of a dealership. It had very low miles for it being three years old. I had the intuitive feeling that it had been in an accident, but I also felt that it was the car for us. I instantly was drawn to it. I test drove it and purchased it on the spot. Soon Luna was talking to a boy "imaginary" playmate whenever we drove in the van. Luna would tell us the boy was sitting in the back seat with one or two of our other family members. The boy was mentioned more and more often, so Enny and I decided to connect with the boy to find out who he was. It turned out our van had been in an accident. The boy in the van was killed in that accident. He already had moved to the light but was drawn to our two children and us. He quickly made friends with Luna and began driving with us whenever the van was used. He was very friendly and entertained the two children whenever we would go on trips. Luna would be talking away throughout the journey and would occasionally relay the conversation to us in the front seat. The boy was a good friend to the children as well as a good distraction during the trips.

Another noteworthy event included Enny's father, Soewono. He crossed over in 1995, two years before Luna was born. When she was three years old, she began to talk about her grandfather visiting her quite often in her dreams as well as playing with her in her room. Enny was pregnant with Mesa so much of our attention was on the pregnancy and birth. Luna spent time in her room playing, and we asked our guides and loved ones to help watch over her. One day after Luna had told us again that her grandfather had visited her, Enny pulled out a wedding photo that had many family members in it. She asked Luna to pick out the person with whom she had been playing. Her finger went directly to Enny's father. Until that time, she had never seen that photo or any picture of him because we did not have many pictures with him in it. We knew from talking to Soewono that he had been playing with Luna, but her identification confirmed it on a physical level.

We did the same thing again after my aunt, Terry, crossed over. Mesa was born by that time and was about a year and a half old. Luna and Mesa kept saying their Aunt Terry was visiting them. We would hear them playing in their room and would hear various names of our family members come up. Once again, we got out a picture of my aunt with various other family members in it, and they both pointed to her at the same time in recognition. Enny was in constant contact with our family members who had crossed over into spirit so she had known the girls were playing with them, but again the physical confirmation was important.

My brother Mark also has played an important role in my children's lives. Although he crossed over in 1961, he has been a wonderful uncle to Luna and Mesa. When the children woke up from their sleep, there were many stories of them playing with their uncle in a tree house, or riding ponies, or playing various games. There have been times when the girls independently have relayed the same events on the same evening of their dreams. Mark had been playing with both of them in their dream state. Other times they would see Mark in the house sitting on a couch, walking through the house, or standing in a doorway. When Mesa was four, she relayed the fact that Mark was like an invisible person that could walk right through doors and walls. She was right.

Luna and Mesa also relayed times when they were sick and their aunts and uncles and other loved ones came to help them in their healing process. They told us about family members who gave them loving and healing energies to help make them feel better and get healthy more quickly. They also spoke of seeing angels around their beds and in their dreams. Having loved ones help during these times is very common not only with children, but also with anyone who is physically ill or emotionally distraught.

It is important that we allow our children to interact with their child play-mates and family members that want to visit. We should encourage it as well as elicit responses and stories of their experiences. In this way, the children are more apt to maintain their openness throughout their lifetimes. We should not be afraid of these visitors, but welcome those who are there for our children's best interests. In this way, they can share in the beauty of interacting with their grand-parents, aunts, uncles, and siblings even after they are no longer physically present. They can be great baby-sitters and teachers to our children and help us out when we ask. Protecting the room with light and love is important to ensure the highest energy vibration of the visitors. Like putting a seat belt on in a car, psychic protection should be used as a precaution without allowing fear to block these interactions. Just as fear of a car crash does not stop us from going on trips or driving around town, interaction with the spirit world by our children should not end because of the same types of anxieties. This area is covered more in the psychic protection chapter of this book.

Helping others discover their spirit guides has always been rewarding for me and those with whom I have the pleasure to work. The results are always positive and very interesting. On one occasion, I was working with a woman named Ash-ley who had started her spiritual path and desired connections with her teacher guides. As we sat and talked, her first guide came through. She was a woman from India. She showed me rocks heating in a fire and then placed them in a bronze bowl. She took aromatic herbs and/or flower petals in water and poured it over the hot rocks. The resulting steam came up, and she inhaled the mixture. Depending on the ingredients, the results were either for healing of respiratory illnesses or for aromatherapy. I asked Ashley if she had been working with aroma-therapy or herbs, and she replied she had been studying both. Ashley found she had an affinity to working with herbs and essential oils, and her learning was pro-gressing quickly.

Shortly after, her second guide came through. She was bathed in green light. Surrounding her were many flowers, plants, vines, and butterflies. Humming-birds buzzed around her. She let me know her purpose was to help with gardening and growing plants. I asked Ashley if she had been interested in gardening, and she confirmed that indeed she had begun gardening that spring. It was an activity that helped her release stress and ground herself. She now knew who had been helping her grow her lovely flowers and abundant vegetables.

Another instance I will relay was when I was working with a client named Melanie. As we talked, her guides came forward. They were a mix of animal and human guides. The first was her grandmother. She stepped forward in a white wedding gown. I received the message that it had to do with Melanie and her relationship with her husband. It was important for her to reexamine her marriage and to not get too complacent about it. I asked her about this, and she explained that she had gotten a similar message from an intuitive she recently had visited. We discussed this for a while and decided it was important that she begin to find ways to rekindle the spark in her marriage of fourteen years.

At this point in the conversation, I felt the presence of another guide coming forward. His name was Oota, and he was a traditional South American Indian rainforest native. He showed me pictures of the couple going on vacation and rekindling their marriage. I asked Melanie if she was planning a vacation. She confirmed that they were planning a trip to Florida. I asked if she had thought about somewhere in South or Central America, but she had not. As I told her about Oota, she was intrigued with the possibilities that such a trip would bring. She loved to cycle and was looking for an adventure. As the conversation progressed, she decided to talk to her husband about a rainforest bicycling trip to Costa Rica, as it was a place she had thought about visiting.

The last guide that came forward that evening was an animal guide. It was a multicolored parrot. I told Melanie that parrots relate to color and color healing. Pleasantly surprised, she told me she had just purchased Ted Andrews' *How To Heal With Color* book and was in the midst of reading it. She was very interested in integrating color into her own personal healing as well as working with others with color. She resonated to color healing and all the benefits it can give. The parrot was there to help her in her studies.

The last session I am going to relay in this chapter was with a woman named Claire. She was interested in connecting to her guides because she was making some life changes and was looking for some guidance. She recently had taken Reiki 1. This was part of a spiritual transition for her. The awakening she was experiencing was all new to her, and she was intrigued about the notion of spirit guides. She wanted to discover hers so she could work more closely with them.

The first guide that came forward was a Native American Indian woman from the Osage Tribe. She did not give her name, but she showed me a scene as she worked with beads and crafts. I asked Claire if she was beginning to work with any beading or crafts, and she exclaimed that she recently had signed up for a beading class. She also was looking to express herself more artistically with craft-type activities. Her guide was a teacher guide to help her create crafts more easily.

Another guide then stepped forward. He told me his name was Wu Shu. He was a Tibetan Buddhist monk. He also was a teacher guide. He was with Claire to help her find peace through meditation. He showed me Claire driving in traffic and how it made her stressed out. I asked Claire about it, and she somewhat reluctantly explained that she was a very aggressive driver. She liked to get where she was going quickly. Any form of traffic or delays put a lot of stress on her. We talked about it for a while, and I gave her some tips to help her during those times to keep her from getting so stressed. We talked about making it a more enjoyable experience by living in the moment and taking advantage of it with CDs that would educate or entertain. Wu Shu also was there to help her with her meditation. She also had been very interested in beginning meditation so she could have a calmer mind. Her guide was there to help her integrate that into her life.

Lastly, an earth guide came forward very similar to the one that came forward for Ashley in the previous story. She radiated green healing energies and had plants, flowers, and butterflies all around her. She stated that she was with Claire to help her reconnect to the earth. She showed me the zoo and the animals. I asked Claire if she frequented the zoo, and she stated that she went there quite often. She actually was planning to go in the next few days. She lived in Canada, and the zoo in her city was one that many people in the area enjoyed visiting. It was a place in the middle of the city that had a calming, natural environment that she could go to and reconnect. Her green earth guide was there to help her with her reconnection, even though she lived in a concrete jungle without too many areas of natural beauty. Claire also liked to take walks and did frequent some of the parks in the area. We discussed ways in which she could take advantage of that time for meditation and stress reduction. After the session was complete, Claire was very excited at the new information she had gained and was ready to use it to help change her life for the better.

No matter what method each person chooses to use, whether singly or in concert, connecting to the spirit guides that are with us each day can be an incredibly fulfilling part of our lives. The veils of uncertainty and fear begin to melt away as knowledge and enlightenment take their place. Order replaces chaos. The knowledge of who our guides are or, at the minimum, realization that they are there to help, is extremely freeing. Taking the time to do this will enrich each day and help to guide us more fully on our life's path and ultimately to higher development and a state of being.

6

The Beauty of Angels

Enny and I began working with angels shortly after we started working with spirit guides. Through our experiences together, and by working with other people and their angels, we have been given quite a lot of information about them. I am not going to recite what others have written about angels, but I will relay what we have experienced and been told by angels about themselves.

Some people confuse angels with spirit guides or loved ones who have crossed over. I have heard many times phrases such as, "My grandfather has crossed over, and now he is an angel watching over me." People also mistake children who have crossed into spirit as becoming angels. Angels have told us that they have never been in physical, third dimensional form. They exist in a different plane of existence but have been known to appear in our dimensional plane. There are many stories of angelic sightings by people throughout history. Some may be delusional, others hoaxes, but some are authentic and real.

Angels are often associated with Christianity, but they have no religious affiliations. They do not choose one side over another. They choose all. They are a direct creation from God and are here on this planet and exist throughout the universe to help those in need. As we look on this planet and its history, we definitely have needed help. They are here to help guide us without living our life for us. Before we come to this planet in physical form, we choose our life's purpose that needs to be fulfilled. Each one of us is given an angel to be with us from the moment of our birth until the time of our crossing back into spirit. They are assigned to us and never leave our side during our waking hours. They accept us for who and what we are. They accept us no matter what we have done during our lifetime. They are pure, unconditional love and do not harbor any type of judgment.

Angels are true guides for our life. Often we hear the voice of reason in our head. That is the path of our life's purpose. Too often, we do not listen to that advice and, after long hours of thinking and justification, we do the exact opposite or try to manipulate events so that they turn out differently. However, as each of us knows, when we do the opposite of what our common sense tells us to do, no matter how difficult that advice may be to follow, life gets exceedingly rocky for us. This is because we have turned away from our chosen life's path. This is free will, and it is an important factor in our existence. Angels cannot change our free will. They can only help give us the advice to try to keep us on track.

Angels are respectful of life and soul experience. They know, as we do deep down, that as humans we are here to experience life in a physical form. Angels know our life path and the pitfalls we will encounter along the way. They will help us but will almost never physically change events to bring about a different outcome. For example, a person has a strong desire to become an acupuncturist/herbalist. This may take many years of studying and practice to be able to do it well. It takes a lot of work. This person may pray and ask that this happen for them. The person's angels may help through a series of events and bring them to a teacher that will resonate to and help them get there more easily. However, their angel will not, no matter how much they pray or ask for it, change wrong answers on the test to right ones or change their grades because they did not study for their exams. Their angel may help to guide them to students of a like mind, thus providing them with a support structure in their learning. Their angel may help them intuitively with clients to help solve difficult scenarios, thus providing an effective treatment for them, but this is through knowledge that the practitioner already has stored in their brain. Their angel may work with other angels and spirit guides behind the scenes to bring clients to them, but they will not appear in a group of people and say, "Go see John Smith for all your health needs. He is a fantastic acupuncturist/herbalist." I am sure there are many people with businesses who wish it did work that way.

We may have more than one angel with us at one time. These extra angels change over time depending on our growth and our life path. However, we do have one main angel that stays with us always. People have equated this one angel as our "Guardian Angel." This angel has many other functions besides just guarding us. They are our primary contact to the angelic realms and also may be a liaison to other higher realms. All angels are there for us during the difficult times, such as the death of a loved one or during a difficult break up of a love relationship. During these difficult times, especially if we ask, many angels will come to our aid and be with us. There is no limit to the number of angels for which we can ask. We are all worthy of the unconditional love angels have to give to us. Each and every one of us is worthy of the attention and love of angels. If there is one thing that Enny and I have heard over and over again while working with clients and their angels is that the angels love each and every one of us, regardless of our social or economic status, mental competence, or things that we have done, no matter how selfish or self-centered that may be. They love us and will continue to love us no matter what.

Angels can work with us in our own healing and the healing of others. There are many stories throughout history of people encountering angels and being miraculously healed. There are stories in current literature of people calling upon angels to help them or a loved one, then are surrounded by a white light presence, and are healed of all afflictions. At the right time and place, angels are able to greatly accelerate our body's own healing processes. Often times, this dramatically changes the life path of an individual through the unconditional love and light of God that is ever present. After this change, the healed person may be once again back on their life's course to teach and share with others their experiences.

There are different hierarchies of angels. Archangels hold a position in a third dimensional framework above those of our main guardian angels. Some that are most closely tied to our earth are Michael, Uriel, Gabrielle, and Raphael. Michael is the archangel of protection, Uriel of emotional healing, Gabrielle of expression and artistic endeavors, and Raphael of healing and being healed. Archangels are able to work with millions of people at once. Because of their high vibrational nature, time and space are not issues for them. They can be in millions of places simultaneously, helping all in need. Each person on this planet should never feel he or she is not worthy of an angel's attention. If help is needed, it is just a matter of asking for it. They will be there. Many times, we have worked with others or had healing circles where we asked for their presence during our prayers or healing work. Sure enough, there they were, adding incredible energies to lighten the spirits of those in need and helping create a powerful environment for healing on all levels.

I began to interact with angels as I studied and read about them. Through meditation, I intentioned connecting to them and asking for guidance. I would get flashes of light behind my eye, intuitive visions, and help with questions that would arise in my life. One day, as I was doing a Reiki session on a client, I had my eyes closed and appearing before me were several white lights that swirled and danced around. They moved down to my hands and lighted on my fingertips. I felt a great surge of energies come into me and then through me to the person with whom I was working. After the session, the client told me that they had felt this surge of energies as well. During the session, I was unaware of the purpose of these lights but knew there was great healing power from them.

Afterwards I reflected and meditated. I asked what these energies were, and I learned that they were a manifestation of angelic healing energies brought forward from angels assigned to me to enhance my healing abilities. The angels stayed with me for several months, enhancing my Reiki techniques and vibrational energies. Shortly after I received my Reiki master attunement, they left, though I could call upon them any time if I was working with a particularly difficult client. They would help me to remove deep down trapped energies or help to relax a nervous client or one that had been through some traumatic event and needed extra healing energies.

I began to perceive angels in a more complex manner. Until then, they always had come to me as glowing white lights. Once they began to work with me in a healing capacity, I began to connect with them on many other levels, but particularly to help me with my own enlightenment and energetic vibration. I was able to perceive them around others, but not in the complex way that occurred later on in my life and development. As I began to perceive spiritual energies surrounding a person, I would interpret their presence as a white light or glowing white ball standing behind the person. In almost all the people that I worked with to connect them with their guides, I saw this white glowing energy denoting their angel standing behind them. In the cases where I did not see this, it was not because their angel was not there, but it was often because the people put up a wall around themselves so that I could not perceive them. This signified to me that they were not ready to hear about the presence of their angel.

There are unique instances in which I have perceived angels not as white light beings but as purple or violet energies. These are the Violet Flame Angels. In late 1998, I was introduced to a CD that was dedicated to sonic tools of healing. Through sound, different energetic states can be achieved to help with healing, chakra opening, or connecting to different realms. On one track, there was music and sounds to help synch and bring in the Transmuting Violet Flame Angels. They exist to help cleanse our bodies and spirits of karmic accumulations, open our chakras, and to balance our beings on not only the physical level, but also the spiritual and etheric levels. I started by relaxing my whole body and doing some deep breathing exercises and some light meditation. I turned on the track with the music, and let it do its thing.

As the CD began, I suddenly was enveloped in a bright, purple light. I felt the presence of two beings, each one on either side of me. They were bathed in a deep amethyst purple light. They circled me in a clockwise direction, increasing the energetic vibrations around me. The light energies also began to rotate in a clockwise direction. The rate of their rotation increased, as did the energies. My body, mind, and spirit were alight with an incredibly powerful feeling. I felt light, as if I could almost levitate off the floor. I could feel a powerful release throughout my body. Every nerve was tingling as energies coursed through me. The energy, coupled with the release, was wonderful. There are no words to describe the feeling I had for those few moments. The tears began streaming down my face from the powerful cleansing and love that emanated from these beings. The CD track only lasted several minutes, but it felt like it was much longer due to the intensity. As the music subsided, so did the energies. Noticing my body again, I realized I was standing on the tips of my toes; arms stretched outward, and my face pointing upward toward the sky. The feeling and intensity was totally unexpected. I felt cleansed and renewed as I put my arms down and sat in the nearest chair. The violet angels had gone, as had the intensity of the moment. I heartily thanked them for their presence and their aid in my personal healing. I received a response not in words but in feeling, "We are happy to help you in our way. Call on us whenever you need us." Since then, I have called on them many times to bring their intense purple healing energies not only for myself, but also for others who are open to the experience. As with all angels, they only have to be asked, and they will come to help heal and show how much each of us is loved.

As Enny and I developed our intuitive skills, we were able to interact with angels on a more clairaudient and clairsentient manner, being able to hear and see them more completely. The first piece of information that came through for us were the names for Enny's and my angel. Enny's angel had taken the name Elizabeth, and mine was Lady of Trust. The name for my angel was fairly straightforward. She said that one of the things she was working on most with me was my ability to not only trust the messages I was given, but to also trust myself and my abilities. This is a constant theme I find with many people. The information is there, but we question it too much. The initial information that flashes through our head is the correct information. As the seconds pass, we begin to question that information or try to make it fit within our framework of experience. This is true especially when working with other people. My angel was primarily focusing on getting me to trust more of what I saw, felt, and experienced and making communication from the spirit world more accurate. I had begun this journey in 1998, but even still, four years later, I was questioning certain aspects of the work. This was making my path more difficult than it needed to be.

Soon Enny and I discovered that angel names have meaning for why they are with us. We realized that we needed to look at the origin, or etymology, of the name and look deeper than just the name itself. For example, the meaning of Elizabeth actually has its origin in the Hebrew language. It originated as Elisheba, which means, "God is my oath." This not only pertains to Elizabeth the Angel, who is a God-centered being, but also to Enny, because she has dedicated this life to working with healing, channeling, and many other forms of God-centered energies for the people of this planet. She had given herself to God.

The more we worked with people and their angels, the more we found how important the names were in relation to that person, no matter how strange they seemed initially. As part of our online work with people, we would help others connect with their angel or their angel would step forward during a Reiki session. As this would occur with clients online, I would relay the information to them. Doing distance sessions was part of what Lady of Trust was working on with me; to completely trust the information given without any prior knowledge of the person with whom we were working.

In the following example, I connected with a woman named Pat online who I began doing distance Reiki sessions on to help with stress and some other health issues. She was the owner of a parrot and exotic bird store. After several sessions, she discussed the results we were having with her parents, William and Mariah, both in their elder years. William was having many complex health issues that were potentially life-threatening, and Mariah had a lot of stress associated with the uncertainty of her husband's future. They decided to try Reiki. The results were positive for both of them, and they decided to continue weekly or biweekly sessions.

The e-mails went through their daughter, as the parents were not computer savvy and relied on her to be the go-between. I would write up the results of the session, and she would print it up and give it to her parents or, if she was out of town, she would read it to them over the phone. After a few sessions, both of the parents' angels came through. I initially had to explain our work with angels and the meaning of the names to relate to them. Every time I would newly connect with someone's angel, there was always a lot of happiness, love, and joy, not only on my end, but also on the angel's end as well. That is easy to understand, as they have been with a person for many years helping out, never being recognized, until one day someone on the earth plane sees them and is able to relay a message for them. Here is an excerpt from the original e-mails that we sent to each other.

In my e-mail after the session I wrote:

"Lately, Enny and I have been able to connect with each person's guardian angel. Tonight, both of yours came through and let themselves be known. Here is the info:

For you, William, your angel's name is Harold. Now I know you may be think-ing, 'What the heck kind of name is that for an angel?' But Enny and I have found that angels have had many names throughout their time associating with people. Their names are ones that we can relate to. You need to look at the ety-mology of the name.

Harold is derived from Old English, Here and Weald. 'Here' meaning Army, and 'weald' meaning ruler or leader.

This somehow relates to you. Our angels have these names to relate to what we have chosen to become in this life. For you, it may not be an actual army, but it may be more figurative. It is directed towards you, so I cannot give a direct answer until I get some feedback from you.

For Mariah, her angel's name is Evelyn.

Evelyn comes from English and was originally derived from Avila. Avila is the medieval Latinized form of Avis. Avis is associated with the Latin word for 'bird.'

Because of all your work feeding and working with baby birds, this one needs no explanation!

Your angels both had a combined message for me to relay to you:

Both your Angels have stated they are proud of the path you have taken throughout your lives. They want you to not be afraid or depressed. As we get older in this society, we fear that which we have lost, youth, and also the loss of our body as we return to spirit. They want you to know they are with you now and will be with you at that time in your life to return to spiritual form. They say to keep doing what you are doing, to be happy, and enjoy each day. Keeping the positive attitude will greatly extend your physical existence so that you can enjoy the fruits that you have manifested in your lives, and to continue to enjoy each other's company and the company of your family. Take the time to enjoy it all and continue taking care of yourselves to have a long and healthy future."

The next day I received an e-mail from Pat:

"Oh My Gosh! You made me cry! In a good way! I haven't faxed this to my par-ents yet; I just wanted to tell you how right-on you are right away!

My dad retired as a sergeant first class Army Ranger after 20 years. My husband said he was a ranger back when rangers were the real tough guys. Dad never talked about the military stuff with us, as I was born right after he retired from the Army. My husband Jeff was an Air Force captain, so he is able to get my dad talking about his past a little bit. My husband thinks highly of my dad and respects him so much.

I wanted to thank you for all the great work you have been doing with my parents!"

I continued to work with all of them, with the outcome of each session always improving. Every time we worked together, there was a close connection with their angels and other family members that had crossed over. It was always a wonderful experience when we were brought together.

There are two more stories that I would like to share involving angels. The first involves Enny and my angel, Lady of Trust. One evening she gave Enny a message to write on a piece of paper and hide it from me. The next morning as I got dressed for work and finished putting all my clothes on, Enny, half-asleep, told me to look in the bedside table for a note. I went over, got the note, and opened it up. On it were the exact words that described what I was wearing! Enny explained to me that my angel had given her that information the night before. I was impressed!

The next evening Enny wrote on a piece of paper and told me not to look at it. The morning came, and I went over to our closet to get ready for work. This time Enny told me to not put the clothes on but to choose what I would wear and place them on the bed after I had made my decision, with her in view the whole time. This was to ensure that I saw that she had not written anything while I was choosing my clothes. I took the pants, and then, as I reached for the shirt I was going to wear, I suddenly decided to change my mind, reached into the middle of a pile of shirts, and pulled out one that I rarely wore. I placed them on the bed, feeling triumphant that I had not been the victim of fate but had used my free will to change the future. As I opened the piece of paper, the clothes that I had lying on the bed were written there. I threw my hands up, and Enny and I both laughed!

Enny said she would do it one more time. Once again, the next day I woke up and, in getting ready for work, chose my clothes. I already had resigned myself to the fact that what was written on the page would be what I placed on the bed. Sure enough, I opened the paper and there was written the clothes that were lying on the bed. I looked around and said to Lady of Trust, "OK, you have made your point!"

This episode showed that our angels indeed have foresight into our future. This gives them the ability to help guide us to where we need to be. Angels do not perceive time as we do, but are really more "part" of time than experiencing it as it occurs in third dimensional reality.

The second episode happened in April of 2003. I felt that I had come quite a long way in terms of trust than when I started back in 1998. I had done thousands of Reiki sessions, both in person and distance, and had connected with numerous angels; spirit guides, nature spirits, and many other beings. I felt confident in my abilities to trust the information that came through. I talked with Lady of Trust about this and asked if there was another name she would like to be called. I heard it loud and clear, "Susan." So, I went online and looked up the name Susan and was quite surprised. Susan is a short form of Susanna, which is derived from Sousanna, the Greek form of the Hebrew word Shoshannah, meaning Lilly. It hit me that where we lived, and where Moonglow was located, was on Lillie Road. Everything had all come full circle. Lady of Trust/Susan/Lilly had helped guide me to our location on Lillie Road. It was all too perfect!

People often ask their angels for protection. I have discovered through personal interaction that angels will help protect us from some occurrences, and others they will let happen. They may even encourage moments of what may be considered at the time negative experiences. Angels are not here to protect us from everything. There is much that we still need to learn or have happen to us due to karmic circumstances. If we are negative in our actions and the way we treat other people, and then we ask our angels to protect us from anything similar happening to us, that is something that is usually not likely to occur. Our angels are here to help us learn on many levels. "Bad" things may have to happen to us so that later in life we have personal experience to help others or to deal with similar circumstances in a more enlightened manner. Angels are here to help us down our path in life, not live our lives or shield us from negativity that we, in fact, may create ourselves. What they will do is continue to love us and continually try to help us, even if we shun their advice repeatedly and pretend they do not exist. They will help us with the same situation one hundred times, hoping that by the one hundred first time their advice will be taken. They know what each person's life path is, even if they have lost their way. They will always help guide in the right direction. They hope that someday they will be seen and given thanks for their presence. Even if a person does not know who his or her angels are, they can take a moment each day and thank them for the help that has been given. Throughout the day, if we each can pause for just one moment and give them thanks, we will be one step further toward discovering who they are: wonderful, beautiful, and loving beings.

7

Where Am I Going? Crossing Over and the Afterlife

Throughout the time that Enny and I have been working with our spirit guides, angels, and many other spiritual contacts, a picture began to take shape, becoming clearer over time as to what the afterlife is like. I am going to focus on the plane of existence closest to our own human one and where most of the people on this planet end up after they shed their physical bodies. There are higher planes of existence beyond that, but I want to focus on those most immediate to our own. I believe that has the most relevance and interest for us as humans.

The physical body ceases to function when the ties that bind the physical to the spiritual is severed. Many people believe that when the physical body quits, the spirit is released. It is actually the opposite. When it is time for the spirit to leave the body, it is then that the body ceases to function. This has been proven many times as people who were thought to be physically dead have returned to perfect health. One common example is someone trapped in cold or freezing water for hours. After resuscitation and physical medical care, the person fully recovers and lives a long life. Some people are able to sustain incredibly damaging trauma that would normally kill many others, and then heal and pull through. The difference was that it was not their time. The karmic laws that bind our physical to our spiritual essences were followed. Not until it is truly our time will our physical and spiritual ties be cut.

The physical realm that we inhabit on earth is actually one of lower vibration and subject to many physical and natural laws. For example, to travel from New York to Paris going a certain speed will get you there in a certain amount of time. Spatial distances are covered in seconds, minutes, and hours. At this point in our development, we need to build vehicles to get us from one place to another more quickly. We are limited by fuel consumption, economics, scheduling, and many other factors. We have to contend with danger to the physical body from crashes, effects from emissions, and faulty construction. In the higher realms, there are no such limitations or dangers.

When illustrating the plane of existence above this one, I am going to do it in a way that includes all of us, because many of us are from there and will return there. For sake of definition, I will use the term "spiritual planes," but in the realm adjacent to ours, it is as much solid and real to those existing there as life here is to each of us. In the spiritual realms, we are able to manifest what we need and desire. God generates unlimited amounts of energy for this to happen. The universe is one of abundance not only in material wealth, but also in love. Too often, we focus on that which is material, not realizing that these attachments are what keep us reincarnating again and again in the earth plane. The ultimate goal is to develop so that these desires are no longer a central part of our being. Each time we return to earth, we are given the chance to create a higher vibration for our souls so that we ultimately can stay in the spiritual planes and develop more fully, gradually working our way closer to becoming one with God. Most people that we encounter are interested in what happens immediately after physical death and then beyond. I will have to answer in generalities as each person has his or her own unique experiences. These experiences come from their own beliefs as they went through life and their expectations of the afterlife. Our experiences on earth may dictate what our after-this-life experiences will be. I will cover the most common experiences that have been related to Enny and I and also what we have experienced while working with many who already have crossed to the other side.

The predominant experience that we have been told, especially through loved ones who have crossed over, is a positive one. Just before moving out of the physical body, other loved ones will come to give help and comfort through the process. They surround the person with their presences as well as generate vast amounts of love and affection to help calm and reassure. Many times our belief systems gained while on earth make this an anxious event. Those that we have known throughout life who have already made the journey create a joyous environment to make the transition as easy as possible. This is a time of homecoming and is treated as such. People present during the crossing over of a loved one often have reported them talking to family members long gone. They may hold long conversations with people seemingly not there. They are not talking to illusionary or phantom people. Those in the spiritual realms actually are there helping to prepare their family member or friend for the journey.

Soon after being greeted by friends and family, a doorway opens that connects the lower spiritual realms to the higher. I call this "stepping into the light." It is the pathway connecting to the higher vibrational energies that represent what

God has to offer us, unlimited and unconditional love. It is the pathway to healing and of higher purpose. No one is excluded from this opportunity. As the person steps into the illuminating light, they begin the transformation and journey into the higher spiritual planes. Not everyone takes it, which will be discussed later in this chapter, but it is offered to each and every person on the planet

After we enter the realms of light, balance begins to be restored. All memories are retained. There is no loss of personality or any other vital information that makes us unique. If we were sick with a long illness, this is instantly healed. Any imperfections that existed in the physical body are erased. The spiritual body is one of perfection. It is exactly the same in all characteristics, but it is perfect in form and function. If the person was elderly, a more youthful appearance may be donned. The spiritual body is lighter and no longer encumbered by the weight of the physical body. This allows freedom of movement to anywhere a person may want to go.

My brother Mark has been a close spirit guide for Enny and me. He crossed over after only two days of planetary incarnation. One day Enny was talking to him and was making many inquiries as to the process of crossing over. Mark decided to show her through direct experience. Enny and I both understand she was given this knowledge so that we could share it with others.

The morning after talking to Mark, Enny was awoken to the state between sleep and wakefulness. Mark took her by the hand, and she was raised out of her body. She was not afraid, because Mark had explained the nature of the journey. Initially, it was dark. No light appeared at all. Then he guided her to a shaft of light that led to a huge tunnel. She was taken through this tunnel for several moments until she reached the end where two shining white beings awaited on either side. They identified themselves as angels. Enny stated later they were both wearing white robes but did not have the wings that we perceive angels have. It was explained that there are many forms of these high vibrational beings. Enny passed between them and into a great hall. There were slots holding books that went as far as her perceptions could capture. Each book held the records of a person's life. It was explained to her that at this point the person is given a complete life review. In this review, each individual is shown every second of their life as they lived it on earth. The person is required to look at it critically from a point of view of unconditional love and forgiveness. Each one of us is asked to forgive ourselves for each wrong that we have done to others. This includes unkind words and actions that have directly and indirectly hurt others. If we have lived lives of destruction and pain toward others for our own personal gain, then this forgiveness may take some time to achieve. If we lived a life of love and service to others, and went out of our way to help, then our path to forgiveness is much shorter. Healing and enlightenment occurs much quicker for the person who has done loving and caring deeds throughout his or her lifetime. For some, this forgiveness may take years. Depending on the life each person leads, this forgiveness may take one or more lifetimes to fully heal the soul. This healing occurs as the person does good deeds or follows an earthly life of service to others.

After the time spent in the Hall of Records, Enny was taken back through the tunnel and into her body. Shortly after her experience, she relayed to me all that had happened and her thoughts and feelings. It was explained that she was given this experience so that it could be relayed to others to help ease the fears of those still troubled by the uncertainty of death. Many others also have taken this journey to help strengthen the message that death is not an end point but a continuation of a cycle that is repeated many times for each of us.

Through talking with those who have crossed over, experiences can differ. Some people are met by loved ones and then step into a white light gateway and are taken. Others are met by angels and are taken into the light. Still others, not yet willing to move forward, wander the earth spending time with the loved ones that they left behind. The time people can stay in this transitional state varies as to the decision of the person who is in the process of completely crossing over. Some people may take years to move into the light, preferring to hang around familiar homes, people, or neighborhoods.

Once the person has moved into the light, they are then able to interact freely with loved ones that already have made the journey, as well as move about the planet at will and visit anywhere they choose. They may visit places on earth that they always have wanted to go but never had the time or money. They may visit loved ones still on the earth plane and see how their lives are going. Still others may choose to travel to other places around the earth, solar systems, or galaxies once they are able to intention their travels in this manner. From what Enny and I have gathered, this takes some practice and guidance to do but, once learned, is fairly easy.

The physical characteristics of the person remain in a form that is desired. If the persona of a younger person is chosen, the physical characteristics of that persona will be seen. If being an elder is the physical choice, then the person is as they were when they were older. The outward appearances of a person are no longer as important as they were in the physical world. This is because perceptions are much different. People see each other as they truly are, not as they appear to be. Once in the higher dimensional planes, speech is not necessarily needed. Most ideas are transmitted through thoughts and intentions. The awareness of each person varies but, typically, each person is seen as his or her spiritual energies project. If a person was a selfish and avaricious person on earth and recently has crossed over, then that will show in their energetic field. If they were a kind person, helping others, that also will show up for all to see. Everyone will be seen for their true selves and be loved unconditionally. Each person around them will try to help them heal and forgive all that was done to others while in physicality. We are all connected, and that becomes apparent in the spiritual realms. Each person knows this and helps others to achieve peace and forgiveness before they have to come back to earth to live another life.

Our senses while on earth change dramatically when we cross over into spirit. The desires that we have while in physical form are greatly reduced. Eating, drinking, and breathing are not needed, because there is no gross physical vessel that needs these items. We exist on life force energy that abounds throughout the cosmos. These physical needs and desires are what we are attempting to be free. We are all reaching for the time when these attachments are no longer necessary. The desire for the taste of food and drink, tobacco, and other worldly attachments are what we all need to release to move upward in our journey to the Source. It is often easier said than done. Many lifetimes are needed for us to accomplish this. If someone wants to eat and drink, then that is available. If someone wants to sit and watch movies all the time, they can do that as well. Whatever we liked to do on earth, we can manifest it. Many others learn new skills and knowledge. This will help them when they choose to return to earth. Retained knowledge will be locked away in the higher self that will be accessible when returning to earth. This becomes apparent for those who return and have a natural ability toward a skill or life path. This can come from past life experience as well as information gained between physical lives.

One activity that seems to be common is family and friends getting together and spending a lot of time with one another. It is a time for the renewal of relationships and the creation of new ones. Other information I have discovered is that entertainers continue to perform for others. Large venue halls are created in which a performer can feature old favorites as well as newly created songs, plays, and other works of art. With all the talent available and plenty of time for artistic endeavors, there is never a shortage of venues to visit.

Those who were well known also are accessible by those able to connect to them. An example of this occurred one evening while Enny and I were in our bed late at night. We just had started channeling many family members and friends. Enny had begun to be clairaudient and clairsentient. She could hold a conversation as if the person was sitting next to her in physical form. Chris Farley from

Saturday Night Live fame was one of my favorite comedians. I was saddened when he crossed over. I asked Enny if she could connect with him so we could say hello and to see if he actually would come through. It only took a few moments, and Enny made contact with him. She relayed that his outward appearance had changed, and he was no longer the heavyset person he had been in life. He explained that he was spending much of his time hanging out with the other Saturday Night Live cast that had crossed over. They were all having fun among themselves as well as performing for others. They were having a great time. It was at this point that Phil Hartman also came through to say hello. Enny and I were pleasantly surprised to be talking to both of them. Through the brief conversation we had, Chris Farley actually was the one who first told me that I was going to write this book and that I should get started. I had no intentions at that time to write but, after that conversation, I began to seriously consider it. We spent about five minutes talking to them and asking questions about their lives, what they were currently doing, and what it was like from their point of view. For all you fans out there, they are both doing great, they are performing for many people, and they continue to help others heal through their ability to make others laugh.

This all seems so earthlike and, in many ways, it is. However, in many ways it is not. It is a different plane of existence. People do bring many of their preferences with them from earth, but part of the time spent in the spiritual realms is about letting go and discovering new areas of interest. We are able to use our psychic senses much more than our physical ones. We are able to communicate with others via thoughts and visions. Misunderstandings do not exist because ideas are relayed much more clearly and do not use language as we do on earth. As stated before, travel is much easier, even to the point of visiting other worlds. However, it seems as though most people still are tied to the earth plane and have to return even though they may not want to.

Another big difference is manifestation of needs and desires. On earth, we need to work or somehow procure money to buy the things we need. A home, food, clothing, etc. are all needed for survival. In the spiritual realms, manifestation is accomplished by thought. The life force and creative energies generated by God are used to form those things we desire. They are held together by the will of our thoughts. When we are finished with them, they return to energy to be used for something else. For example, if a person always wanted to own a large Cadillac, it can be created through intention and visualization. If someone wanted to live in the house he or she had as a child, it can be created from thought. A large mansion can just as easily be manifested. Once again, though, it is these types of attachments to physical goods that keep us coming back to earth. Many souls choose to study and learn higher vibrational lessons to further their ascension toward God.

A good real world example came from working with a client, Allen, who had liver cancer. He later became a good friend due to the bond we forged while he was in physical form. We worked with him for many months. Through intention and will, he was able to extend his life and quality of life for more than six months. He was an avid golfer and played until he succumbed to a coma at the end of his physical life. Throughout his coma, we were able to stay connected to him and relay messages to his family. When the time came for him to cross over, we again stayed connected and helped him through it. When he was on the other side, he told us that he was doing a lot of golfing. I asked him about that issue. If he was able to manifest anything he wanted, couldn't he just manifest a hole in one every time? He told me that he could, but that it would be boring. It was set up to mimic the game on earth. However, he stated, there were some people who, when they crossed over, did such things as hit holes in one constantly. They also manifested lots of gold, money, and other material and needless things. These were people who did not have much abundance in their physical life. Once they got their fill of frivolous materialism and progressed, that type of behavior was left behind. Allen liked to golf and also fish and made sure that he manifested conditions such as those he experienced on earth to make it a challenge. Allen continues to touch base with us occasionally to say hello and sometimes add his voice of knowledge.

Allen also was able to interact and help his common-law wife, Theresa, whom he left behind. She was emotionally devastated when Allen left. He was instrumental in helping her to heal. Initially, she had trouble connecting with him, but soon he was appearing in her dreams and letting her know he was all right. We also conveyed messages to her from him. One of those messages was of his attempts to help connect her to a new man who would help her with her healing as well as be a companion and friend. Soon she had a man come into her life and help her heal from the loss of Allen. Several months after Allen had crossed over, she was expressing her knowledge that she would once again connect with him in the spiritual realms, and she knew he was with her when she needed him. The loving connection continued even after the separation of the physical form.

This is an important topic that I have found imperative to relay to others. Even after physical death, the bond of love connects us. This bond is very powerful and can stay with us for many lifetimes. As our loved ones cross over, leaving us to continue our journeys on earth, they can be called upon in times of need.

This has been very apparent with my brother Mark and us. He has helped Enny and me on many occasions. He has relayed messages for us, given us valuable information as well as encouragement to improve our lives, and helped make us better at what we do. He has helped my mother heal from the trauma of losing him. When she opened to his presence, he came to her in dreams to let her know he is doing great and continues to interact with her, even if she may not feel his presence.

Other family members also have helped us. My grandfather, who was very good in business, has helped us with advice that also has aided in our ability to do more with the abundance we receive. Since we have been doing this work, several of our close family members have crossed over. As each one moves into the light, they join our family that already is present. They often come to our house to gather and talk, adding their voice of wisdom and knowledge. Mark has become our gatekeeper spirit guide. He is the single voice that represents the many voices in decisions or information that is given to us. It is always of a higher nature, helping us to become more God-centered to help those in need.

Many people on this planet have become very disconnected from their loved ones as they cross over. Because of this loss of spiritual awareness, they lose their connection to those that have crossed the veil into spirit. The loss creates great emotional and psychological issues that can take years or are never healed. As awareness returns to those searching, the emotional responses to physical death are like night and day. It becomes more of a celebration than a loss. This is especially true when long terminal illness and pain preceded the passing.

Mark once came to Enny in a dream. She saw him and me playing basketball in a gym surrounded by glass walls. Before the game, we shook hands. We began to play, laughing and enjoying ourselves. After a short period, he took the ball, and instead of shooting it into the basket, he threw it into the wall of glass. It broke into a million pieces. After waking, Enny asked Mark the meaning of this dream. He told her this is what was being asked of both her and me, to break the wall of glass that separates the spiritual from the physical. Together, with he representing the spiritual realms, and Enny and I the physical, this book was going to be used to aid in breaking down the barriers between the two.

I believe that it is up to each of us to begin to shatter the wall of glass separating us from not only those we have known and loved, but also our angels and guides who continually help us fulfill our life purpose. It is important for people living in Westernized societies and those who have taken on Western values to reconnect to the spiritual aspect of the death process. Realizing that the spiritual essence lives on and the bonds of love prevail will dramatically lessen the trauma and fear of losing those we love. Light and love will enter where sadness and fear once existed.

People in comas also are an interesting topic. Because of the amount of cancer and other diseases that have become a part of our society, comas have become more common. In this state of being, the spirit leaves the body and, while still attached, is able to travel. Often the person in the coma is in the same room while family and friends visit, talk, etc. Many times health care providers will encourage people to talk to the people in the coma. Upon waking, the patients are able to relate information about what was said. This is because that person was present in the room while the events occurred, only in astral form. However, there are limitations to which the coma patient must adhere. They are not disconnected yet from the physical body; they still are tied to it. So, they are in a limbo existence; they are not able to move into the light, but not able to use their physical body either. They stay in this situation until either they wake from the coma or the physical/spiritual bond is severed. If the person awakens, they may view their time in the coma as a dream or may remember the event as astral traveling and have full recall. The ability to connect loved ones to people in comas is one that is sorely needed in our society. We have worked with people in comas and their loved ones who worry about them. Being there throughout the process as the person is unconscious for days at a time before they leave their physical bodies behind has done wonders about understanding the life and physical death process. It makes the letting go and healing of those left behind much easier and quicker. When the loved ones left behind are asked to organize a funeral service, it is one of celebration and homecoming rather than one of grief-stricken loss. The differences between these two types of funerals are vast indeed.

The development of removing the veils that exist between the physical and spiritual worlds can take years of study. Beginning the process and achieving results can take but a week. Dreams, use of spiritual mediums, teachers, CDs, and books can all help achieve results. The effort is worth it. So much guidance and knowledge is lost because connections cannot be made between the two. The separation is becoming thinner as more people open their hearts and minds to the existence of the spiritual realms and how the parts involved play in our lives. Beyond this veil is unlimited knowledge and unconditional love. Having access is like being wrapped in a warm, protective blanket that also shares insight and hope to all that take the time to connect and be a part of it.

8

I Feel Like I Have Been Here Before: Past Lives and Reincarnation

It is my experience that we all have lived before, many, many times. In this chapter, I am going to relay several experiences with past life work that Enny and I have done, as well as give some conclusions as to the purpose of past lives as opposed to having only one physical life. These conclusions have come after working with many people in this capacity, as well as through information given to me through my spirit guides, angels, and other people's guides.

I have been asked many times the true meaning of our life on this planet. Much has been written on this subject throughout the millenniums. To me, the purpose of life seems fairly basic. Our goal as individual souls, however simple or complex it is viewed, is to learn and to grow. In this learning and growth process, our souls change. Each life adds to our total being. We never lose who we are or who we were. All the incarnations are stored within our "higher self" who, while we are in physical form, has been unattainable for most of us. The ultimate goal throughout all our lifetimes tied to the earth plane is to become experienced enough so that one day we do not have to come back again in physical, third dimensional form. How long this takes is up to each individual and the karma they attain through each lifetime. Someone who lived their lives concentrated on spiritual development, such as coming back again and again as a priest, monk, yogi, etc., will attain a state of pure enlightenment long before someone who wants to come back and live a life that involves constantly striving for material wealth, glory in battles, or revels in the more basic pleasures that this world has to offer. Once a person can begin to detach himself or herself from the earthly pleasures and desires that drive most of us, then he or she no longer has to reincarnate into the third dimensional plane. They can move upward into the higher dimensions as they have become unencumbered by worldly attachments. This is replayed again in a higher dimension, with lives being much longer and, we as spiritual beings, having much more freedom and knowledge to grow even closer to the God source. Ultimately through the millions or billions of years of evolutions that our souls go through, we will meld with the Creator, still keeping our own individual identities but being part of the "All" the Creator represents.

That is a basic view of life and the meaning of it. However, I think we create many difficulties and make life much harder than it needs to be. I believe that thoughts create and all thoughts on this planet are connected. We as people help to mold and shape our reality. Ideas, new inventions, religious dogmas and beliefs, and communication (or lack thereof) shape the way we view the world. This view, in turn, shapes the way we interact with each other. Most important, this worldview shapes our relationship with the Creator. Someone who believes in one life as opposed to multiple lives may or may not live their lives differently. I have had many conversations with people who wholly believe in past lives, and those who believe in one life. Deep down the goals are the same. Live by whatever spiritual beliefs each one of us has, respect each other as people, and live connected to the source of all things, striving for spiritual perfection and release of earthly confines. How each person goes about that varies greatly. That is the wonderful thing about free will; we are able to choose our path, without one path being the only way to reach our goal. We are given many choices and many paths to walk. Too many people who know far too little about the other person's choices are too willing to tell others that their way is the only way, and everyone else must fall in line or suffer some sort of grave consequences.

Consider, for example, one hundred exact replicas of Jesus, or Mohammed, or Krishna, each speaking differently about how to reach the ultimate with similar ideals but different methods. Each replica represents the different sects of each religion as it has developed over time. Each will claim that adherence to their dictates is the only way to ultimate salvation. Which one do you choose? Some people choose none and follow their own path. Others choose based on how they were reared and ideas to which they were exposed as a child. Some people bounce back and forth between them, trying to figure out the confusing differences and never actually settle on any one. Others look at all of them and realize that they are all potential doorways to reach spiritual enlightenment. I consider myself to be the latter. Throughout my travels on this planet, I have prayed in churches, mosques, temples, and holy sites. I have given thanks on beaches, in forests, on deserts-anywhere the spirit moved me to do so. We have been given the gift of free will and have also been blessed throughout time by enlightened individuals and groups that have given us written guides to help us achieve spiritual enlightenment and spiritual peace. Having this can help us to translate how we perceive the world around us as either hostile and barren or peaceful and full of abundance.

Knowing about past lives can be a double-edged sword. On the one hand, it gives us some insight into the issues needing to be resolved in our current life that were not in our past life or lives. On the flipside, it also can be used as an excuse why things always go wrong for a certain person or why their life is so negative. I feel that past life information is given to us so that we may work on resolving issues from our past. If we can take the information, work with it for our own healing, empowerment, or knowledge, it can help us in our overall soul growth so we can move on and grow. Using it as an excuse will only create more issues, actually sending that person backwards in their path. Past life information that is used by anyone, especially for ourselves about ourselves, should be utilized with a positive goal in mind.

The Akashic Records of a person are all that a person has been, said, and done throughout all of their lifetimes. They are stored in a separate plane from the one we inhabit in our conscious and wakeful hours. These records can be accessed. All it takes is some time and energy, as well as guidance, to connect to them and get the information. For me, the accessing of the Akashic Records did not start off too easily and was really facilitated by Enny. She would do long meditations and connect with people's spirit guides while helping them with their healing and sending distance Reiki. It began while Enny was spending long hours interacting and sending Reiki to my aunt who had terminal cancer. My aunt wanted to believe in alternative methods, but the societal pressure and the draw of Western medicine was too strong for her. She asked for our help throughout her journey of illness and spiritual release. As Enny tuned into her deeply, scenes began to play before her. Enny was told by her guides these were scenes from her past life. This also happened again when Enny was sending Reiki to my father. She came to me after and told me what had happened. I was elated for Enny! This was a big break through for her. The long hours of meditation and work had paid off in an unexpected way. She began to do it consciously with everyone she worked on, asking their guides and higher self for permission. In almost all cases, Enny was shown a comprehensive picture of their past lives, often their most recent life first. The most recent past life was tied in with their present life and issues that may have needed healing.

Enny and I have experienced discovering our own past lives, and it has helped us with our growth and development, as well as our relationship. When the information began to come to us, a larger picture unfolded, and it helped us understand our relationship to one another and our children. To give a more complete picture of how our past lives have influenced our current, I will give a little history of our relationship in this lifetime, and then connect it to our past lifetimes.

I first met Enny in Indonesia in 1990 when a friend of mine, Joe, and I took a trip through Southeast Asia for vacation. We were to spend a month traveling from Papua New Guinea, through Indonesia, to Singapore, Malaysia, and Thailand. The first stop after Vanimo in Papua New Guinea was Jayapura, Indonesia, which was just across the PNG border. It was the destination for many expatriates on the west side of PNG because it was a quick plane ride but a completely different world. The first hour after we had landed, I met Enny. She was the first English-speaking person I met. She was working at the Matoa Hotel as a receptionist. Many people knew Enny because she also was a tour guide for the expatriates that came through. I was quickly attracted to her beauty and warm smile, and soon asked her out for dinner. It was customary for her to bring friends to chaperone, so I took her and two other friends out that evening. I was only planning to stay for a week and then move on with our trip. We quickly became interested in each other and, after a couple long nights of conversation, we realized that we were really connecting on a deep level. After a week, I rescheduled our trip to come back after two weeks to spend another week before returning to PNG.

For two weeks, Joe and I traveled through many countries. Soon we were back in Jayapura, and Enny and I discovered during the next week that we were in love. Indonesian custom does not dictate long dating, and soon we began talking about marriage. I thought it was love at first sight, but it was actually a rekindling of the many lives we had lived together. We discussed marriage with her parents, and they were not too happy about her daughter marrying an American. Since I still had four months left before my contract was over with Peace Corps, I knew there would be time to think about this on my end, as well as hers.

The four months passed quickly. We had a lot of correspondence in that time not only between her and I, but also with her family and religious leaders. When I returned to Jayapura four months later, everything was organized. Within six days, we were married. We had spent a total of three weeks together in person before we were betrothed. That is a short time by much of the modern day world's standards. I returned to the U.S. several weeks later, and Enny followed in three months after all the paperwork and visas were completed.

Enny and I have worked together on our spiritual path, balancing each other out. Her strengths are my weaknesses and vice versa. We work well together. We have known each other in many lives, but this is the first one that we have been together as husband and wife. In our previous incarnations, she was the wife of my business partner. Our business was successful and made us wealthy. However, the partnership did have some problems and caused some animosity between us. The life before that Enny and I followed a religious path. We were both high-ranking Christian clergy. I was Enny's superior. In that situation, there also were some issues, and I had to discipline Enny, which once again led to some animosity between us. This animosity did materialize itself in this lifetime as well. There were some issues of competition and some underlying tension that we were not able to identify. Over time, we did discover the reasons, and we were able to work on them, letting them go and clearing the way for us to move forward. In this case, our past life information helped us to grow in the present.

I have been able to uncover other past lives of mine. Some were with the help of Enny and others, and some were shown to me. I can trace my lives back to both Greece and Rome. Several of my lives a little more than two thousand years ago were ones of great privilege and power. Because of my status in society, I felt I could treat others badly. I accumulated much bad karma and had to change my route. I soon chose a path of spiritual awakening. For the last two thousand years or so, I have followed a spiritual path. I have been an East Indian yogi, a Buddhist monk, and a Native American Indian shaman. I mostly have lived with few material goods, shunning them for poverty and spiritual growth. In the last two, I have had material wealth as well as spiritual. This lifetime I am also blessed with great abundance in terms of spiritual knowledge, friends, family, career, and experiences. I am doing what I have trained many lifetimes, sharing my spiritual knowledge to help others attain the skills and empowerment that I have received. It is my karmic path to do so, and I will continue on this path until it is time for my spiritual essence to disconnect from my physical.

I would like to continue in this chapter about other issues relating to past life work and how its knowledge can help us grow as individuals. I have learned throughout the years an important lesson about judgment of others. On this planet, judgment of other people is a big part of our societies and plays a big role in how we interact with each other across racial, geographical, political, and social boundaries. Having knowledge of past life information, there is an important lesson to be learned. We all have been, at one time or another in our development, that person or group of people we are judging. When seeing a person lying on the street, destitute from alcoholism that has led to homelessness, there is a good chance we were once that type of person. The woman who takes money for sex to survive was a past life we may have lived. We also all have lived lives of privilege and wealth. The point here is that we were all rich and poor, fat and thin, ugly and beautiful, intelligent and slow. It is all part of growth and development. So when walking down the street and an unwashed and unshaven destitute man asks for money, and a remark is made, such as "get a job" or "freakin' bum," we have just judged not only them, but also ourselves. We all have been a variety of people. If someone dislikes black people, they may have been black once or many times. If someone does not like white or Asian people, remember that in one or many lifetimes, they may have lived in Asia or may have once been a slave owner. It is karma.

Enny and I have connected with many past lives of many people. There is often a recurring theme. Most people come back as a person opposite of the life or lives they just lived. Rich people come back with less money, white people were once black, people who treated Native American Indians badly came back to live on a reservation. Not only is this done to atone for some of the wrongs that were done, but also to experience the full gamut that life on this planet has to offer. When saying or thinking derogatory things about others that don't meet up to our ideal of what we think a human should be, remember we once may have been much like that person. To judge another person is to judge ourselves. To put down others for their ethnicity, religious beliefs, or their body type is to put ourselves down. It is all part of the interconnectedness that God created on this planet, and it is part of the lessons that we must learn before we can stop reincarnating on this earth. Our souls will have no true and inner peace, as well as no long-term growth, until each and every one of us living here can come to terms that we all are each other, and each other is us. A good strategy to begin to change from a position of judgment to one of unconditional love is by seeing each other in a different way. Next time while walking down the street and noticing someone who instantly springs a judgment or derogatory comment to mind or lips, look into the center of their chest. Instead of viewing the person before you, see the glowing white God essence that is their true self. In seeing that true white light essence, know the form that person has taken is only temporary. Help them with their experiences and growth, as each of us would like others to do for us along our journey. In doing so, the light will shine brighter and the path will be less cumbersome for each one of us.

Another recurring issue is the connectedness to family members through various lifetimes. Groups of souls travel together through time, changing their roles within the familial structure. Fathers in one life may become the son in another. Mothers and daughters may switch places. All the possible combinations that can occur do. We support each other through different lifetimes because we are connected by love. We want to be there for each other to help through the lifetimes.

The earth is truly a school of hard knocks, and each of us can use all the help we can get. As we experience different lifetimes in different forms representing different ethnic groups and geographical locations, we stay within the group for support. Those whose souls grow and mature more quickly help others in the family group to ascend through their actions and combined wisdom. In doing so, the family group is able to draw upon the strengths and learn from the weaknesses of each other.

Genders also may change through lifetimes. Someone who was a woman in one life may be a man in the next and vice versa. The transition may not be complete or past-life orientation may come through strongly into the next life creating sexual confusion. This confusion manifests itself in same sex orientation as well as transgender lifestyles. It is important that we do not judge people going through this transition. They are on their own journey, and it is up to us to help them with their full experiences. It is very possible that as each of us has strived to experience both the male and female forms of being human, there may have been instances of having the same difficulties. We need to treat each person as an individual expressing their unique form among the infinite possibilities of the universe.

As soon as Enny and I developed our past life talents, we began offering past life readings through Moonglow. Many of the clients that I had previously worked with doing Reiki loved the new skill I had acquired. They began asking for information pertaining to their past lives. I gladly obliged. By that point, most of the people would go through the regular Reiki session and ask for the information. Early on, I was working with a woman named Dawn who connected at the same time and saw everything that I did.

Dawn was a white female in her early forties. I had been working with her steadily for about two months via distance Reiki sessions, so we had a good connection. She had just gotten her PhD., so she was well educated. As the past life session progressed, I saw scenes of an African-American woman cleaning a large house. She had on a black dress with white lace trim. The period was mid- to late-1800s. The man she worked for was a military officer, and I saw him plainly standing in his blue uniform. At one point, the woman who was once Dawn, walked straight up to me and showed herself top to bottom by rotating so I could see everything about her. She looked at me and smiled. I first thought it was a spirit guide with Dawn, but then I got a clear message that it was Dawn in her most recent past life. After the session, I relayed all the information to Dawn, and, soon after, she wrote back to me:

"Keith,

You are not going to believe this! I saw an African-American woman clearly tonight! She had a round face (mine is oval) and was dressed in a black dress (Me NEVER IN A DRESS!) with a white head covering (ME A BANDANA MAYBE!). At first, I thought maybe she was a nun, but she bared her head, looked down slowly, and calmly raised her head. I felt her looking me straight in the eyes! This is so wonderful! I did not know for sure, but felt it when our eyes connected. She did have large eyes like me, but hers were brown and mine are blue. She also seemed to be about 5'2," and I am 5'8." I initially thought maybe I had a different guide moving in the picture! I love to do this!!! Thanks so much, you are a gem to me!"

Dawn's previous life was one of servitude without any formal higher education. She was an African-American woman that was born before or during the civil war and lived as an adult shortly after. She lived in a northern city and was not a slave, but certainly being a woman and black at that time, she did not have many rights as a person. Her life was lived in servitude to others.

In her current life, she was highly educated and a teacher at a university. She was independent and enjoyed any of the rights enjoyed by the rest of society. She chose a life opposite from the one she had before. There were still many lessons to learn in this lifetime, but they were different. She enjoyed helping others to learn, and she was looked up to as a teacher and someone that had a lot of knowledge. Knowing her past helped her to appreciate her present life. It helped her to focus more on teaching others so they, too, would have more choices in their lives.

The main issue that impressed me about the session was that she experienced the same thing at the same time as I did. This was important for me. It gave me a huge confirmation that I needed and also a great boost of confidence. Before that, I often wondered if I was making the scenes up in my head or were creating them to fill some preconceived notions of what I was supposed to do without actually doing it. The session gave me much help with the issue of trust. I knew what I was seeing with Dawn and the other people I had worked with up to that point was real, but there was no way to actually prove it.

This was an important lesson and one that I pass on to all those I teach. Receiving accurate information during past life connecting comes from practice and trusting in the information that is given. There is no real way at this time in our development to scientifically prove the information we receive. It mostly comes from confirmation with the person with which we are working. Trusting the information is crucial to continuing on with this skill. The information that comes forward initially is what is most accurate. For those searching for their own past life information, during sleep or meditation scenes may come through that seem familiar but are from a different time. This is most probably past life information. As we intention the information to come forward, it will. We all have the ability to access our Akashic Records.

Part of the difficulty with confirming accuracy is that rarely do any names come through, and, if so, only first names. It would be much easier if the name Fred Johnson who was born in Boston in 1888 came through during the sessions, but it never does. I have asked other mediums that do past life work, and they all say or write the same thing, that getting full names almost never happens. It has to do with concentrating on our present life and not dwelling on the past. If we all had the knowledge of who we were, then we would spend far too much time looking to relive the past in some sort of nostalgic way and forget about the work that needs to be done in our present. This would be too detrimental to the growth of most of us and would create yet another obstacle in our path.

Another memorable session that I experienced occurred shortly after working with Dawn. I was doing a dual distance Reiki/past life session with a new client. I met her via e-mail, knew nothing about her except her name, and went from there. As the session began, I saw an alternating blue/white light passing behind my eyes. I was unsure why, but put it down as a mental note. The colors then changed to bright oranges, yellows, and greens. This went on for several moments and then began to solidify into a woman dancing and wearing an extremely bright-colored dress. The origin was South America, and I clearly heard "Colombia." The dates I was given for birth was 1880 and physical death was in 1932. The cause came due to a stroke.

The woman was dancing in the middle of a town square on some traditional Spanish mosaic tile. There was a band behind her and spectators watching and moving to the lively rhythm. Socio-economically, she was considered lower middle class. She was married and had a husband that owned a store/cantina. There were two children, a boy and a girl, and a third that was either miscarried or aborted through herbal means, most probably the latter. She loved to be the center of attention and did not mind a kiss now and then from a stranger or someone with money. I saw her life go from horse drawn carriages to automobiles, but she was not economically able to afford a car. She was of Spanish descent and was proud of her heritage. A lot of time and money was spent partying and entertaining. The one main message that came from all this was that she liked to dance and dance and dance! It was her true passion.

Shortly after I relayed all of this information, she wrote back:

"I have always had a natural ability with dancing, particularly to African and Latin rhythms that seem to betray my Anglo-Irish appearance. I was raised 'secular American' but converted to Judaism at 19. I love dancing and don't do it as often as I would like to and used to love the attention I would get for it. As a young child, I remember dancing with a friend who had years of dance lessons and her family being keenly aware that I danced better, though I had never had any lessons.

I just took a class on Latin American poetry, and there was a lady in the class from Columbia that I was quite drawn to. Aha! It was all fascinating! A thousand thanks!"

Sometimes during the sessions, I see things, such as the blue and white colors that were not immediately apparent to me, so I needed feedback. The colors, blue and white, related to the fact that she had converted to Judaism early in life. The flag of Israel is blue and white. This is the difference between the distance and the in-person sessions. With the distance sessions, I go with the information I receive, give it to the client all at once, and then wait for the feedback. When someone is sitting with me or I am talking to them over the phone, I get the feedback immediately and am able to move deeper into the session. I had developed my talents so that I could delve deeper into the past life information and come up with much more complete details. All the information is there, it is just a matter of accessing it and deciphering it.

In other cases, I have found that there are similarities within past lives or events that carry over from life to life that affect the present situation. This was apparent to me when I did a session with a woman named Charlene. The first life I picked up on was of her in Prussia ending in 1862. She was a man and a cavalry officer during the Prussian Expansion. The one scene that came through most vividly was of a battle raging all around me. I witnessed barrages of cannon and gunfire, with men and horses screaming. It was quite intense. In the midst of battle, he took a bullet to the throat and died on the battlefield. I saw this replayed three times before the scene shifted.

The next was altogether different. It was of a time and place in America. This time in her life, she was a woman, a housewife. It was in Danbury, Ohio, and the time was the 1930s. Her husband was a banker, and she had two children, a boy and a girl. They lived in a typical large wooden house of the time. It was an opposite life than the one before it. She was quite unhappy. I got a great sense of melancholy, of dreams unfulfilled, and of a household full of control and not of love. She had a hard time expressing herself. She also smoked many cigarettes. This dependence on cigarettes helped create the physical manifestation of the throat cancer that took her life. She was forty-two years old. Once again, the throat was a centerpiece of her physical death.

After I gave her the information about the session and her past life, she responded with:

"Quite an amazing experience. I've always had problems in my throat, definitely emotional related. When I get backed into a corner and feel I can't possibly tell a person how I really feel, I get a 'knot' in my throat. When I first started Reiki classes, I almost reached a point of not wanting anyone to work on me because every Reiki session created enormous tension in my throat. As the subject of the group's distant practice, I was placed in the middle of the room and thought the tension in my throat, which felt like a rubber band pulled to its tightest, was going to slingshot me into another world! So, yes, it is my biggest block. I am grateful for this insight and healing, as this was the first session where I didn't experience my throat tightening.

Before the session, I prepared my environment with the vibrations of healing Reiki and did a healing self-treatment on myself. I did have some thoughts of a young girl who was controlled by her husband, caught in a situation she didn't think she could escape from, and resigned to a life where she was not allowed to speak for herself.

As I seek to trust God and myself, all these happenings are accepted most gratefully."

Charlene discovered that the issues she had with her throat, Throat Chakra, and the inability to express herself had some deep roots into her past lives and her manner of death. Once these issues came to light, then it was easier to work with them and resolve them.

Working with the higher self and the higher self of others also can help bring information that can have dramatic effects. In August of 2002, Enny and I went to Auburn, Washington to the annual Light Workers Campout. There was an event there that opened a doorway of knowledge that was important in my understanding of the higher self, past lives, current lives, and channeling.

A speaker and famous trance medium, William Rainen, was scheduled to speak and channel Dr. Charles-James Andrew Peebles. Dr. Peebles was raised in

Scotland, learned allopathic medicine in England, and came to the U.S. to practice in San Francisco until the time of his physical death in 1902. Dr. Peebles had a straightforward, witty personality that endeared me to him almost immediately as he spoke through William Rainen that day. Throughout the session, audience members were encouraged to ask questions either about Dr. Peebles' life or details about the spirit world, reincarnation, or past lives. The question came up about the higher self and accessing different personalities within the higher self through channeling. The answer to the question was quite informative and, as it all unfolded, it literally blew me away.

Dr. Peebles explained in his own entertaining way that the higher self contains all the information and all the personalities that we have been throughout our lifetimes. If someone was a Native American Indian warrior back in 1745 and had since reincarnated two, three, or four times, through trance mediumship that personality could be accessed. That person could be talked to and interacted with as if they were in the room having a regular conversation. This is because they are, in a sense, present. This is part of the complexity of the higher self. None of the people each person has been ever really dies. They become part of the higher self, a multilateral being that is hard to imagine existing in our third dimensional, single-minded existence.

This complexity of the higher self explains why we can connect to famous people, or anyone for that matter, that once existed long ago and have since reincarnated. Once the vibrations can be matched with those of others existing in the now or previously reincarnated person, connection and communication with just about anyone that has ever existed throughout history can occur. Dr. Peebles explained that in his previous incarnation before he was a doctor, he was a tribesman living in Africa. This tribesman whom he was could be communicated with just as Dr. Peebles was being communicated with, and at the same time. It is possible to connect with the ancient past to the Egyptian Pharaoh Tuthmosis III, as well as Uncle Phil that recently had crossed over. It is just a matter of gaining the skill and having the reason to connect with whatever person chosen to reach out to. Free will exists on both sides of the veil, and communication may not occur if there is no deep connection or mutual agreement. There needs to be a reason, either apparent or subliminal, before that connection will be made.

For me, the question of whether we live one life or many lives has been answered. We live many lives. The exact number is different for each person. I find it hard to believe that an unconditionally loving God, with an eternity to exist, would put such stipulations and restrictions on us and still expect us to grow and mature as beings in one lifetime. The time span of one human life, even if it is the longest ever recorded in human history, is but a mili-instant to God and time. To have only one lifetime surrounded by extremely divergent and confusing viewpoints on the nature of God, sin, and the afterlife is way too short. It is my understanding that the growth and development we are going through on earth also has happened on countless numbers of planets before ours. The universe is billions of years old. Human history, even if you consider what some scientists would say were our most basic ancestors that go back one million years, is still a mere fraction of time next to the age of the whole universe. As humans, we still are maturing, and we have a long way to go. However, we are working on it, and I believe that we have made some good progress and will continue to do so. God is waiting for that time when we can become part of the universal consciousness.

I believe that what we are going through on this planet is something that we are not alone in experiencing, although we may be unique in the exact way we are doing it. There are four billion stars in our galaxy. There are at least four billion galaxies with billions of stars. Many of those stars have planets with life on them, growing and developing their own sets of experiences. It would be extremely egocentric to think we are the only sentient life forms in the universe. I feel there is a system put in place by God to bring planets from the ignorance of their beginnings into the enlightenment of being a part of a galactic community. We are along in our timeline but still have a ways to go. It is up to us as a planet and a people as to how long that will take.

There are many divergent thoughts about the nature of the beginning earth and of humans. I feel those that believe in *only* creation have it partly right. Those that believe in *only* evolution have it partly right. I think we are somewhere in the middle. God created the world billions of years ago. The planet progressed and matured until one day it was fit for human habitation. Our spiritual essences became physical and expressed themselves as humans. We were left by free will to develop on our own while given all the tools, plants, animals, and whatever else we need to be nurtured through our social infancy. We were created as beings close to God's heart and given a chance to experience, bringing earth and its inhabitants to a higher state of self-awareness. God has made us forget our origins, and then said, "Come find me. I will give you everything you need at your disposal. I will give you as much time and as many lives as it takes for you to return to me and once again be a part of me. I have eternity to wait. I love you with all my heart and will not judge you along your path. All that you do will be part of your experience for you to share and behold. When you are ready, you will return."

So we struggle and fight with each other. We love and caress each other. We study and revel in all we have been given. As we develop along the way, life after life, we begin to know the true nature of God and our desire to return to what we have lost becomes stronger. Some day, as a planet and a people, we will recognize what we have lost, hold one another's hand in worldwide connection, and move forward in peace and harmony. This connection of unconditional love toward one another will enable us to recognize our true nature as humans. Until that time, we will continue to live, leave our physical form, and be reborn to live and learn again. Use this lifetime to the fullest. Send love to each other to bring light to this planet, thus moving us all toward our ultimate goal of sharing in the divine and eternal love from whence we came.

9

Time To Move On: Earthbound Spirits

Earthbound spirits exist throughout the world. They inhabit our homes, businesses, hospitals, churches, and natural environments. Enny and I have encountered many that exist in that state for different reasons. Some feel they are not worthy to move into the light. Others are afraid because of their religious backgrounds. They feel guilty for some perceived sins they had committed and were sure certain damnation awaited them on the other side. Others die violent deaths and, as their spiritual essence leaves their physical body, they are confused and are unsure what their exact status is. We have encountered people that have died in battle and sudden violent deaths, such as car accidents and murder victims. Many others have committed suicide. They are afraid that they may be condemned to hell for their actions or their already low vibrational energies gravitate toward low energy places or people. In all these cases and others, the spiritual consciousness and etheric bodies of these people wander the planet, some being innocuous and others being malicious. The earthbound spirits need to move into the light, not only to heal and become whole, but also because their energies "weigh" the vibrations of the whole planet down. To help bring a more connected peace to this planet and all beings living on it, assisting the spirits into the light aids the earth as a whole. It also raises the overall vibration of the planet and subsequent dimensions.

A friend of mine, Wes, introduced me to the assistance of earthbound spirits. I met Wes while spending time at Randy Shaw's. He had moved onto Randy's property for a short stay while he was working out some personal issues. Wes was staying down by the river that ran through the property. It was a spiritually active area, and Wes was right in the middle of it. He had opened himself up to helping earthbound spirits but had encountered some problems along the way.

92

Many mediums find spirits are nocturnal. They tend to wake us up early in the morning, especially between 2 and 4 AM when most people are deep in sleep. Many spiritual mediums are receptive to connecting with them at this time of the morning. Many times, I have been given some of the most vivid visions at this time as well as some of the most intense connections between the physical and spiritual world. It was this time of the morning that he would be woken up to help call earthbound spirits to him. He would assist them into the light. Sleeplessly, he channeled and helped many that came and requested his assistance. Wes quickly became worn out. He was tired all the time and would try to catch up on his sleep in the daytime, but often that was not practical. After a few months, he had to put an end to it. He felt as though he needed to help in what he was doing and was committed. On the other hand, he was being used, with little regard for his own health and mental well-being. He finally said a loud and emphatic NO to those that had been using him for this purpose. The aid he was able to render was put to an end.

Later, I met a reputable and established medium with a similar story. He allowed himself to be used to help a large number of earthbound spirits to move out of the earth plane. He was a spiritually aware person that went to Manila in the Philippines for a visit. While in a deep meditation, he was asked if he and his body could be used to help clear the city that was densely populated with earthbound spirits. He agreed, not adequately protecting himself, as he was unaware of the magnitude of the undertaking. After assisting approximately twenty thousand souls, he ended up in the hospital for a month. He fully recovered but never let himself be used in that manner again.

It was through these stories and experiences that I told my guides, angels, and the Creator that I did not want to be used in this manner. I valued my health and sanity. I knew the responsibilities of doing that type of work and what it would bring upon my family and me. For about three years, I steered clear of getting involved with any type of work involving spirits that had not moved into the light. I also made sure to put up barriers of protection around our property, house, and especially our bedrooms. I did this by consciously creating a white light barrier of protection around everything. I constantly strengthened this barrier each evening before I went to sleep. It was not fear that caused me to put up these protective walls, but a desire to focus my attentions in other directions. I did not want to be constantly awoken in the middle of the night or have any of my family disturbed. I knew deep down I was not ready to handle the responsibility that went with the task. So instead of doing it incompletely or incorrectly, I decided not to do it at all. I felt it was better left to others more educated to the task then to possibly help some and not be able to help others.

Then, one evening while I was working in my home office, I felt a strong urge to take a break and go outside. I began to make my way over to an area of our property that still was relatively undeveloped and unlit. As I walked toward my destination, I saw and felt a strong presence. In the middle of the circular and unlit fire pit was a bright, glowing, and ethereally flowing light being floating about four feet from the ground. I knew it to be an angel and, upon connecting, realized it to be my angel, Lady of Trust. I asked if there were any messages for me. I was met with silence. I grabbed a nearby chair, sat down, closed my eyes, and was soon bathed in the pure white glow of her energies. It was wonderfully healing and intense. I felt loved and protected. After several minutes, Lady of Trust bade me farewell.

I sat for another five minutes, basking in the afterglow of her presence, when I felt a completely different energy surrounding me. I lifted my head, opened my eyes, and there before me stood a girl of about twelve years old. She had a severe head wound that was pouring blood. I knew immediately that she was in spirit form, because I perceived her with my mind's eye not my physical eyes. It was not the wound that unsettled me, because I had seen many head wounds as an Emergency Medical Technician, but it was the energy she was emitting. It was energy of pure negative emotion toward me, almost considered hatred. She stood there, eyes glaring. I was unsure what to do. I looked beyond her and could feel and see the presence of many other people that had crossed over into spirit but were held back by the barrier of protection I had put up. I could tell they all needed and wanted help but, at that point, I was unsure how to do it without letting an outpouring of spiritual energies into our personal space. I was uncertain how to remove them once they were there. With the girl, I tried everything I knew how to do at the time to help her into the light. I called in angels and my guides to help her. I called on any light beings that could help. I even called in the archangels. None of it worked. After several minutes, I could take no more. I got up from the chair, quite shaken, and moved into the house. Once there, I put up many shields of protection between where I was sitting and our house. She did not follow but stayed outside.

After putting physical distance between her and myself and getting inside where it was fully light, I began to feel much better. There still was the dilemma of helping the young girl out and many of the others who had come in search of aid. For that evening, I resigned myself to the fact that this was beyond me. I would have to seek counsel from another source. It was late in the evening, and the person I was thinking about calling was asleep. I waited until the next day to call her and get some info on how to help move all the spirits around our house into the light.

When I telephoned, I knew she was the right person. She gave me the exact answer I was looking for. I did have the answer all along within myself, but I needed it to be brought to the surface and explained in a way that it could be accomplished safely without using my own physical form as the vehicle. I decided to do it that evening.

Night came and I prepared myself. I burned sage, meditated, and protected my house, the surrounding area, and myself with white God-centered light. The instructions I was given were to do the work inside the house while projecting the doorway into the area through which I intentioned them to move. I visualized the scene and the spot of the previous evening. The fire pit in the middle of the section kept coming to mind. I created a vortex of energy, swirling my hands in a clockwise direction. I saw in my mind white energy coming down from above into the fire pit. I intentioned this to be the doorway they were to step into to be taken or transported. I called in angels, spirit guides, and any other beings of love and light to help with the transition. I was nervous and a little scared but moved forward knowing I was protected. Suddenly, there was a flash of white light, and I felt a powerful presence in the room with me. I had my eyes closed, but the light was almost blinding. My angel, Lady of Trust, stood before me. She handed me what I could only describe as a white, brightly glowing, cut diamond about the size of my head. I heard in my mind, "Take this and use it to move them into the light." I instinctively took it. At that moment, a large rush of energy hit me that almost brought me to my knees. I stood firm, asking those in spirit with me to guide me through the process. I projected the glowing gem into the vortex of light. A "doorway" opened. I could see many people moving forward and into the doorway. There were men, women, and children walking. They had older-style clothing on, as well as contemporary clothes. They all had happy expressions, and some even waved in my direction. I was fixed in place, not able to move, with copious amounts of energy pouring through me. After what seemed like several minutes, the last person walked through. Lady of Trust moved to me again and took the glowing gem from my hands. The energy subsided, and the doorway closed.

I was extremely light-headed from the experience and sat down. My body was highly energized and overly stimulated. It felt as if it was "humming" with energy. I focused and reflected on the circumstances of the last few moments. It was hard to believe what had just happened to me. The implications were enormous, and I knew it. Now that I had the knowledge of how to do this, without using my own body as the conduit, I told God and those there to help in this endeavor that I would continue as often as I could. I knew this was a responsibility I was being called to do. I gratefully took it, knowing the importance of the work before me. I put the intentions out that I needed help, protection, and guidance if I was going to do this on a regular basis. I also knew there were many and varied reasons why people do not move into the light. Some of them were not nice people in life, so they were probably the same if not worse after moving into spirit. I knew some of these people had low vibrational energy. I had to maintain the protection if I was to continue while, at the same time, keeping our home safe from intrusion.

I talked to Enny about my experience, and she intuitively connected to some of the people who had crossed over. They came through strongly and said how grateful they were they had help. Although I had felt the same sentiments as the event occurred, it was not verbalized as strongly as it was to Enny. Many of them initially were frightened to do it. However, when the time was right, they were ready and happy to have the gateway and the powerful energies generated to help them raise their vibrations so they could put aside their fears and move forward. They asked us to do it every day if possible. Those who had moved into the light also were called to go and help others that were wandering in between the worlds and direct them to the doorway. It would become an area where those who needed to could come at any time and be helped.

I began to do it every evening. For the first couple of weeks, I used the glowing gem that was handed to me. After that, the vortex was sufficient in continual energies that I did not need it. I began to shape the area with intentions, creating a unique place for them to come. I knew that our thoughts create, so I formed a new environment in the spiritual realms through meditation and projecting each night. I knew I had to keep the area contained so that mischievous or needy spirits could not enter into where I did not want them disturbing us. I put protection around the doorway and created a hallway to walk through into the vortex of energy. After a couple of months, I created a façade that was made completely of marble, which had two large columns on both sides, stairs leading up, and a large double doorway made of shimmering copper that had embossed on it an angel with her arms open wide.

The number of people who would come each night grew as word got around that it existed. Sometimes I tuned into them moving through the doorway, and I saw people of all cultures. Each night before I opened the door, I sent all the people waiting unconditional love and light. I let them know not to be afraid and, if they were not ready, that the doorway would be opened each night.

I went around the county and began to open temporary doorways. I wanted to help clear out more areas and to draw more people who were afraid. Soon after I began opening the gateways, I was asked by my guides to drive up north to a secluded beach. It was a rocky and a rough drive. After getting out of the car, I had a long walk. The beach I was walking on had a long history of being used by Native American Indian people. I knew that it was going to be a day that was centered on helping them. I was connected strongly to my Native American Indian spirit guides and kept my intentions and my energies focused for the task. I had worked with indigenous people for many years at that point, so I was connected to many Native American Indian people: shamanic, warrior, and others. This was a task I took on eagerly.

I had to climb down a rocky slope to get to the beach. It was an incredibly beautiful and energetic day. As I walked, it felt like a journey that had to be taken. I wanted to just sit and enjoy the surf, the blue sky, and the crystal clean air. However, I knew there was more that needed to be done, so I struck out in the direction I was instructed to go. It was a natural and rugged remote beach. The surf was beginning to come in, and there were areas I had to climb up and over. I had to navigate over streams that had made their way to the ocean and other obstacles. Usually when walking along the beach, I would find beautiful jaspers, white quartz, and other rocks. However, today I knew that the rocks I would be collecting would be used to help open a gateway. I had this image in my mind of what was to occur, but did not have the rocks yet. As I kept walking, they began to appear in the sand. I picked them up and put them in my pocket. I knew that I was to make an energy grid from the stones and then create the vortex with that at the center. An energy grid is made up of any combination of stones in a Star of David configuration and is connected energetically with a crystal or with healing energies such as Reiki. The connecting of the stones creates an energetic environment in the area where the grid is activated.

As I walked, I began picking up some white quartz that was plentiful on the beach. I spotted bright red jasper and picked it up as well. As I walked further, I caught a glimpse of yellow in the surf. I almost passed it up but was physically drawn to turn around and go back for it. As I walked closer, I saw it was a bright yellow large piece of druzy quartz. I never had seen that type of quartz before and intuitively knew it was going to be the centerpiece of the grid. I continued to navigate the beach and another bright red jasper appeared. I now had all the pieces I needed. I placed the druzy quartz in the center, with the two red jaspers and the white quartz around the edges. I did a ritual of protection around myself and then stood back and connected all the stones together using my fingers to channel Reiki energies. As I connected the last stone, I was filled with light energy. I knew it was time to complete the process. I could feel the presence of many spirits around me, and it was an anticipatory energy that was created as I opened the gateway. I had my eyes closed but once again, the white light energies that came in were blinding. I felt spiritual presences passing around me and then moving toward and into the gateway. I brought my hands up and added to the energies. The vibrations were strong, and it left me light-headed. I stood for several minutes until I felt all who needed to use the gateway had done so. I lowered my hands. I did not close the doorway, but kept it open. I knew that where the grid was placed, the doorway would not be open indefinitely as the tide would come up to that spot in several hours. All would be washed away, disrupting the cohesiveness of the doorway and closing it. As I stood there, listening to the surf, I raised my arms, brought in as much energy as I could, and projected it outward in an ever-expanding circle. I desired to call out to all spirits that were trapped to come and use this doorway while it was open. I had hoped to call as many as I could reach to come before the doorway was closed.

It began to get late, the tide was coming up, and I still had a couple of rough miles to walk. I said one last good-bye and thanked all those who had come to that spot. I thanked them for using the doorway or helping in its creation. I took what seemed like a long journey back to the car. Once there, I grounded myself to drive and headed home, happy in the knowledge of what had transpired in that time and place.

Another instance transpired while I was working with a client using distance Reiki. During the session, I connected to two of her guides. These were people she considered as role models for her life. As a proliferate writer, she took pride in being a woman in America. During the session, I felt two spiritual energies come through strongly. The first was a male, and the second a female. I got the first couple letters of the man's name because I heard in my head a strong "O—S" but could not get the rest. My clairaudient skills were just beginning, and names were difficult to figure out. I kept getting a "J" sound for the woman's name but could not get the rest. After the session, I wrote back to the woman and relayed all the information about them. I told her how I had connected with two of her spirit guides and gave her the sounds of the names. It was shortly after that she wrote back and asked me if I knew who Jane Addams and Oscar Wilde were. They were both near and dear to her heart and had been positive role models for her. I did know who Oscar Wilde was, reading several of his works throughout my school years, but I did not know who Jane Addams was. She provided me with a link in the letter to both Jane Addams's and Oscar Wilde's autobiography. I read up on both of them. I found a deep kinship with Jane Addams.

Jane Addams was the first woman Nobel Peace Prize winner. She received it in 1931. She was a pioneer social worker and feminist whose views reached out internationally. She founded Hull House in Chicago, and it was a center of radical and deep social-changing ideas. She was, in her physical life, an incredible woman whose legacy lives on as an inspiration to many.

I knew nothing about her until I began to read and study the work she had done. As I read more and more of not only her written work, but of her deeds and accomplishments, I began to feel and realize we had many similarities in our lives. Geographically, we were both from Illinois, and Hull House is on the near South Side of Chicago where I spent much of my childhood and young adulthood. We both have worked for environmental change within largely economically challenged societies. Her focus was on the working-class immigrant neighborhoods, and I have worked with indigenous peoples. She did a lot of environmental health work by changing the basic thought processes of the day, as I have tried to do throughout my professional life. She loved new ideas and fostered them, as I have always done. The more I read, the more I liked her and began to feel close to her.

I did not quite understand at the time all that was going to be asked of me in connection with Jane Addams, but it would soon all become clear. My mother was going to be married in September, just a few weeks away, and I would be in Chicago. I checked out the book *20 Years at Hull House* written by Jane Addams, so I could get more in depth information about her. As I was sitting in my room reading, I felt a strong energy cover my body. I put the book down, closed my eyes, and let the energies wash over me. I suddenly dropped into a channeling trance, a situation I had been through many times before, and let the information flow to me.

I was standing on a sidewalk, looking down a street. Next to me were gas lamps that were used in the late-1800s and early-1900s before electricity was prevalent. I felt a guiding force moving me down the sidewalk. I looked around at the buildings as I walked. They were poorly constructed houses, mostly made of wood, or brick offices. I realized I was walking down a street that Jane would have frequented. She was showing me scenes from her life environment. I was assaulted by smells of sewage and rotting garbage. I could feel the oppressive environment. Everything seemed dark and dingy. A horse drawn cab pulled up, the door opened, and I got in. It was not a cab that was used to transport the rich and famous. It was one the ordinary working-class person would have used in those days. It smelled of vomit, urine, and dirty, unwashed people. I realized all this was to show me what Jane Addams had worked to change. It was the environment she lived in most of her life. She wanted better public health for what was considered the lower classes of people. She worked for change because of these conditions. Her work prompted her to want to change the world around her. These were far-reaching ideals not only in America, but in Europe as well. She was showing me scenes that I could appreciate. I have worked for similar goals and have similar ideals. Once I understood this, the scenes quickly faded, and I was back in my room, in my present time, with her book in my lap. I was determined to go and see Hull House and get a better connection to Jane than the one I already had.

The days drew nearer to my trip to Chicago, and I was getting excited to arrive. One evening as I was sleeping, the feeling of a presence in the room awakened me. I was in the state between wakefulness and sleep. I could feel the beginnings of a vision coming on. Black-and-white pictures came into view. They were of people, but none I had known. They started off small then would come toward me getting larger and revealing more detail. They flew past my vision quickly for several minutes. There were at least thirty that I viewed during that evening. I got a strong message to remember them. At the time, I had no idea what they were about, but felt strongly there would be much revealed once I got to Hull House. Shortly after the pictures stopped coming into view, I fell back asleep.

A few days later, Enny, our daughters Luna and Mesa, and I were on a plane to Chicago. I would not have a car on this trip, so we were going to be ferried around by family and friends. The wedding was on the weekend, so I decided to go to Hull House that Monday. I was staying on the South Side of Chicago, so I was nearby. It was just a matter of driving to the University of Chicago and Halsted Street to see what was left of Hull House and Jane's legacy.

Arriving on Monday, I was prepared but unsure as to why I was truly there. Up to that point, there had been no real explanation as to the reason I was called to go and why and how everything was coming together so easily to get me there. I parked about two blocks away and began my walk. I had all my physical and psychic senses alert. I wondered if someone was going to appear to me, or if there was going to be some great revelation, another flashback, or any other number of occurrences. I walked up to the door, opened it, and walked in. I took everything in from the sights, sounds, smells, and spiritually energetic feel. It all was put together like a museum. There was a person at the desk as I walked in the door that looked like a University of Chicago student. I was hoping to get upstairs. I got a strong feeling that there was someone or something I needed to see and feel. However, the access was cut off from anyone except staff. Off to my right, a presentation about Jane Addams's life had just begun. There was a small class of university students going through it as part of their curriculum. I walked over to the presentation and sat down. As it went on, I began to feel closer to Jane. I took a couple of silent deep breaths, centered myself, and watched the presentation before me. I began to get a great sense of the building and all the important people that had been through its doors.

After the presentation, there was a tour. I joined the group and went along. I was impressed with all the items that had been preserved. There was much historic energy surrounding everything in the building. At one point, we were shown into an alcove where pictures hung of the many famous people who had stayed there. There was a great rush of energy that traveled down my spine, because before me were the pictures of all the people who had appeared several nights earlier in my vision. Each one of the pictures was a face that had passed before me. I smiled to myself and gave a silent thanks to those who had provided me that vision. Pieces of the puzzle were being presented to me but had not yet come together into a cohesive picture.

Following the tour, we were given freedom to wander the premises. We were asked not to touch anything or take any pictures. That put a huge damper on some of my plans. I brought my digital camera and was going to take photos. The reason given was that many of the items were from private collections, and the people owning the items asked them not to be photographed. I wanted to take pictures due to the affinity for digital photography to capture spiritual phenomenon. I was putting a big message out there to any spiritual energies that wanted to be photographed to come forward. It was important for me to respect the wishes of the museum, so I kept my camera in the bag I carried with me.

I looked around a little more and then went to the front desk to inquire about going upstairs. I was told there were offices upstairs and that it was restricted to staff only. I felt there was something there from the past that still existed in the present. It was as if several of the spiritual inhabitants wanted to show me something that would later prove valuable. I stood there for several moments and thought better of it. What was I going to do, go to the guy at the front desk and say, "Hi, my name is Keith. I have come from Washington state because Jane asked me to come here and check out Hull House. Can I go upstairs and look around?" He would have been quite perplexed and most probably unbelieving. So I let the upstairs idea go and politely thanked him. Looking around one last time, I asked for some enlightenment as to why I was there, but still got no answer. I turned around, walked out the door, and, with a little less bounce in my step, walked back to my car.

I drove back to the South Side with many questions in my head but not many answers. I was perplexed as to why I was given all these clues, such as the pictures, the scenes from the street, and the layout of the house, but no apparent reasons. Everything was burned indelibly into my brain, but not a reason for my presence there or the importance of going to Hull House in the first place. I was happy to go and find out a lot about Jane Addams's life, but to go through all of that and still not have any concrete answers was frustrating.

Later that evening I was sitting by myself reading a little more of Jane's *20 Years at Hull House,* when all at once an intuitive light bulb came on in my head. Jane had become aware of my work helping to move earthbound spirits into the light, and she now wanted me to do it at Hull House. There were earthbound spirits residing there, and they were weighing down the energies. Jane was continuing to do a lot of work throughout the world, with Hull House as her central point. She wanted it to shine as brightly as possible and to help those people still residing there but unwilling to leave. Many were drawn to Hull House after their passing when it was still an active and vibrant place. As pieces of it were slowly torn down, they all began to move into the central house, which was all that remained. It was getting crowded, and those trapped there had to be persuaded to move on. These same people would be asked to help in the work Jane was doing throughout the planet, thus connecting many others to help as well. She did, of course, have many who already were helping her, but the more added to the numbers, the greater the overall good could be done. She was asking me to open a gateway in Hull House to clear it out. It was important for me to go there, so I could see the interior and get the layout of the place, without actually having to do any work within the structure itself. For some reason, she did not want me to do the work while I was in the house.

I prepared myself by doing a brief energetic meditation, wrapping myself in white protective light, and doing some deep, energizing yogic breathing exercises. I sat in a chair, holding Jane's book in my hands. I wrapped Hull House in a pure white God-centered light. I was transported back into Hull House. I now knew what it looked like, so I was able to visualize and be much more a part of it than if I had not visited it earlier that day. As I looked out the windows, all I could see was a bright white light. The whole building was encased in it. Standing before me were many people, some with astonished looks on their faces. I knew many of them did not know they had crossed over into spirit and had been living their lives without this knowledge. It became clear to me why this task needed to be done. Before I spoke, I felt four strong presences in each corner of the house. I mentally asked who they were, and they replied with, "We are the archangels, Michael, Raphael, Gabriel, and Uriel, and we are here to help you in your task." To say the least, I was elated. I had worked with them before, all four together once and separately other times, and was glad for their presence and their energies.

I spoke to those people standing there before me. I told them who I was, why I was there, the date, and it was their time to move into the light. I explained they were in spirit, and their presence was weighing down and holding back other work that needed to be done. There were some incredulous looks on some of their faces, some were happy, and some were frightened. I brought the energies in to open a gateway for them to pass through. It was a shaft of white light that came down from the ceiling and was placed right at the front door. I instructed those who were ready to move forward and step into the etheric doorway. I told them not to be afraid, and that they were going to a place where they could be free and reunited with loved ones. Many instantly began to move into the light. They entered one by one. The numbers became fewer and fewer.

Near the end, there were about twenty people who were not ready to move on. Jane appeared and told them it was their time. I was happy to see her. We were able to interact more easily because we were in similar circumstances in terms of vibration. She had taken the look and persona of her later years, as an older woman. She had a wonderful bright white glow around her. I knew that I also had that glow around me. It did not take much at that point for the others who were reticent to walk into the white gateway, to step forward, and move into it. Soon the room was clear, the work had been completed. The light throughout the building had diminished, and the doorway gone. I thanked the archangels for their help and beautiful, powerful energies. I gave Jane a great big hug, moved out the front doorway, and waved one more time to her as I left, sending her one last dose of unconditional love before I was transported back into my body.

Wiggling my toes and moving my hands, I began to breathe deeply. I opened my eyes and looked around. The top of my head was buzzing and, once again, my body felt like a live wire. I checked the clock, and twenty minutes had passed. All the pieces of the puzzle had fallen into place. The work had been accomplished. Jane Addams was now free to continue her work unencumbered, spreading her love, and helping hands throughout the world. I love you, Jane Addams! You are a shining light in this world.

I have continued to open doorways whenever I travel, especially in the larger cities. Often the amount of earthbound spirits that are drawn to these doorways is tremendous. I have found that in larger cities, the concentration of these spirits is much higher than in the rural areas. Many are tied to the familiar and stay in the same area where they spent their physical existences. I have found them in buildings, old houses, empty lots, restaurants, and many other places. When I am able, I open doorways so that they may make the transition that is needed for them. As long as I am anchored in this physical world, I will continue to open doorways to help those that may be too afraid or not able to find their way into the light.

This activity is light oriented, but not something that would be recommended for most people. Many of the earthbound spirits we have helped have not been of the highest energetic vibration and are looking to create problems while they are in between the worlds. Often it is fear of the unknown, or hell, or other consequences due to their earthly activities that have them in that state in the first place. Some of these individuals are not kind, and some are looking to do harm to others. Sometimes holding out a hand to help makes it a target for such people. We have encountered some but have always known we are protected. This does not mean that we have been without incident. There have been times that we have been attacked while in dream state or have felt the menacing presence of others around us. I have included some of the more dramatic instances in our psychic protection chapter, but I also would like to add some other examples here as well.

First I would recommend that anyone desiring to help others cross into the light fully understand that unless adequate protection is in place, they will leave themselves open to being awoken at night by lost spirits or possibly menaced by others. For those who are called to do it, it will come naturally, and all the information will be given. I have learned from experience that not everyone is adequately prepared for the responsibility of undertaking such a task.

The first example I would like to give that has made me come to this conclusion involves my sister, Mary Ellen. She also is a Reiki practitioner and intuitive and was interested in helping earthbound spirits after we informed her of our activities. We gave her the knowledge on how to do it and also how to protect herself. She lives in a moderate-sized city, so there were plenty of earthbound spirits around needing help. She began to open the doorways and, for a couple of days, all went well. Soon spirits began to be drawn to the positive and healing energy that she created, and they started waking her up at night. The feeling of someone over her bed or watching her would rouse her. Her young three-year-old daughter also was aware and intuitive, and she would be awoken in the middle of the night, talking about the people in her room looking at her. These spirits were not there for their highest good, but instead wanted help. One evening a woman even tried to get into bed with Mary Ellen, but she pushed her out. The woman was an unloved person in life, and as her physical body was severed from the spiritual, she was lost in limbo due to her feelings of unworthiness. Mary Ellen eventually was able to help her, but it was unsettling. It became apparent that Mary Ellen and her family were not ready to take on such an undertaking, and we began working on ways to completely shut the doorways. It took a couple of weeks, but eventually we closed everything down, put up adequate protection, and they were no longer bothered.

Another instance of having earthbound spirits causing problems occurred with my brother, Steve. Soon after Enny and I became aware that earthbound spirits gravitate to people's homes, we started helping to clear them out of all our immediate families' residences. Steve had quite a few that were of low energy because he collected World War II items as well as vintage electronics and societal memorabilia. Many of these spirits resided in the basement of his split level house. Four in particular were intent on staying. We were adamant about them leaving, so it became a test of intentions. We had attempted to remove them without success. The next morning I left for work. Shortly after, Enny heard the back door of our house open, and she thought it was me. She was in the state between wakefulness and sleep and felt the presence of someone malevolent in the house. Through a test of wills, she was able to get the intruding spirit out as well as three others that shortly after attacked her in her dreams. That evening I came home and heard the whole story. It now had come into our home turf, and I was resolved to take care of it in the arena of their choosing, dream state.

That evening before I slept, I intentioned that I would confront them. Through a test of wills, I would help them get out of the current mind set of having to use violence and help them find their way into the environment of love, forgiveness, and healing. I did dream, and they did come. I was able to protect myself and, through a series of events, was able to persuade them to move into the light. The next day we connected with them, and they had indeed done so. They apologized and said they were happy since they had been helped through the doorway. It became their karmic mission to help others find their way. Through their adversity and ours, much was learned and accomplished. On a side note, my brother also had suffered from a recurring dream of a woman who would accost him and squeeze various parts of his anatomy, causing him to wake up in extreme pain. Since we cleared the house of all earthbound spirits, he has not had that dream again.

We have helped clear out houses where children had constant nightmares. Children are much more aware to spiritual energies, and those of a lower energetic nature can be disturbing to them. Other people have felt they were being watched or had recurring dreams that involved them and their houses. They did not feel comfortable, as if someone was there who did not belong. Through our experiences, we have found that earthbound spirits reside in many homes in city environments and less commonly in rural homes. We feel it is important when buying or moving into a new home that it should be cleansed. Older homes should be as well, as they can often have earthbound spirits residing within them. Often these spirits do not mean any harm, they just feel comfortable with the residents who live there and want to share their living space. Unfortunately, they do not belong there and need help to find their way so that they can move forward with their healing and karmic path. Through awareness of their presence, they can be helped to realize that they are worthy to be in the light of the Creator. Finding their way home is imperative.

10

Keep Your Personal Space Clear: Psychic Protection

More than just earthbound spirits can interrupt the serenity of our lives. Negativity can affect us in other ways, too. I feel it is important to always spiritually and emotionally protect ourselves, whether it is to further development of intuitive talents or a negative coworker who seems to suck the energy from everyone around them. It is important for those who are either already undertaking a path of spiritual enlightenment or are about to start, to protect themselves. We take other precautions such as putting on our seat belt when in a moving car, buying insurance for economic protection, or wearing a helmet to ride a bike. It is the same with protecting ourselves from emotional and spiritual attack. I am going to relay some experiences Enny and I have had, but these are far above the norm. These types of occurrences have been rare and have happened to few of the thousands of people with whom we have connected. I think most people have a better chance of being hit by lightning or winning the lottery than having some of the experiences that we have had. We put ourselves on the front lines and, therefore, are more apt to have these experiences. In sharing these experiences, it is not my intention to create fear. I want to help those who may be having issues of spiritual attachment and to help prevent those who are following this path from having it happen to them. Keeping up even a moderate level of protection will help to ensure that most negativity will not be able to affect us. When surrounded with the light and love of God, spirits and beings that do not have our best interest at heart will not be able to be in the same room. Where light shines, darkness shall not enter.

One thing I never have had a problem with since I began this path was the fear of anything harming or negatively influencing me. I always have surrounded myself with light and have felt somewhat like a warrior for God. That may be a bit of a misnomer, as God is much more geared toward love and less on war and fighting. However, I have jumped in the middle of situations never wavering from my path, because I always have known I was protected from harm. I have been guided by light, so I have known that the darker, more selfish energies could not penetrate the protection around me. It has been something innate and never questioned. I believe this is from the many past lives I have had following a spiritual path. So when I was asked to help with someone who was being stalked by a person who had taken darkness as his or her path, I did not hesitate to help.

A co-worker came to me and asked if I would help with a friend of hers who was diagnosed with lung cancer. She had come over from England, spent some time with a Native American Indian tribe in New York state, and, because of some personal issues, had left and come to the West Coast. She did not expect to live long. She was only twenty-six, and the cancer had begun to work its way through her system. The doctors had given her six months to a year to live. She had two small children and probably would not see them grow up. She had been a child star in England but, later in life, had gone to school to become a social worker. Emma came to me, hoping to get some help with her cancer. I began intensive Reiki sessions with her, doing three or four per week. She began to improve rapidly.

I did not know it at the time, but she had married a Native American man in New York in an attempt to stay in the country. For the sake of the story, I will call him Brad. He had talked her into it, hoping that by doing so, she would not be deported because her visa was about to expire. It was a marriage of convenience and not of love. However, there was much more to her story than that. Her husband also was a traditional medicine man, as were other members of his family. Emma began to have things happen to her that she was having trouble explaining. They were events of a dark nature and, as she took me into her confidence, I realized what was occurring.

Two instances took place in which she was almost killed. It began while staying in the home of one of Brad's relatives. She was walking down stairs in the home that led from the upstairs bedrooms to the downstairs living area. From the corner of her eye, she saw a dark shadow then felt a strong push behind her. If she had not been holding onto the banister, she would have gone tumbling down the stairs, greatly injured or even killed. As it was, she tumbled part ways down and did sustain some injuries. She looked around her, and there was no one there. The second time was in the bathroom. Once again, she felt the dark presence as she was leaning over the bathtub to turn off the faucet. She felt a push that slammed her against the wall and into the half-empty tub. If she had been knocked out, she would have drowned in the water. Once again, there was no human present in the room. Throughout this period, she also had been having horrific nightmares. After these two occurrences and the nightmares, she felt as though it was time for her to leave. She had a strong suspicion that it was Brad's aunt and felt she needed to get out of the vicinity. She had suspicions she also was creating the cancer within her. She took a bus with her two children and headed west.

A couple months after she arrived in Taholah, her husband wanted to visit her. She had gotten along well with him in New York, so she decided to agree to his seemingly two-week visit. The family with whom she was staying had approved it. He arrived by bus the following week. I met him two days later on the beach. The moment I met him, I felt a prickling sensation on the back of my neck. Something was not quite right with the whole situation.

Shortly after Brad arrived, she began having the nightmares again. I meditated and tuned into the cause. It was not Brad's aunt but Brad himself. He was the one causing all of the issues. I knew it was time to act. I talked to Emma about my feelings, and she admitted at that point she believed it to be Brad also. I asked her if she had a stone or crystal with her that she could carry in her pocket. She reached around her neck and pulled out a stone on a cord. She told me that during her trip west, a man had given it to her and told her that soon she would need it. It almost was like a movie, in which the all-knowing stranger comes and offers a protective talisman. I then knew there were other forces at work helping to protect Emma. I took the stone and placed some powerful protective energies into it. It was something that Randy Shaw had taught me and I refined it as I gained more knowledge. Not only did I infuse the stone with protective energies, but I intentioned that any negativity or "spells" that he cast upon her would return tenfold to his head, creating headaches. This was before I learned to transmute the energies and return them to the originator as unconditional love.

The moment she walked in the door of the house, he took one look at her and had this crazy look on his face. He walked right up to her and started screaming at her, asking her what she had done and where she had been. He instantly knew by his own training that she had gone to see someone that was working to protect her from him. He knew that he had been discovered. She did not tell him it was I. He thought it was a local native shaman doing the protective rituals for her. The less he knew about me, the better it was for all of us. I could work in anonymity and not worry about him attacking me. He kept trying to break through the protection I had put around her and her children. He paced back and forth all night outside her door, muttering and cursing but could not enter her room.

The next morning it started all over again when she came out of her bedroom. He yelled and screamed at her, wanting to know where she was getting the protection. He kept grabbing his head as if it was about to explode. All of his energies were being returned to him right into his head. I am sure the pain was tremendous with the amount of hatred he was spewing. She left the house and later came to see me. By that time, I had gotten some other ingredients and put them into a medicine bag for her. It was stinky but worked like a charm. When she encountered him again, he was even more furious and unable to do anything to her.

To stay in the house, Brad used his powers to put the man of the household under his influence. It appeared that Brad could do nothing wrong. Brad would take him out nightly and continue to weave his web of deceit. Brad was asked to leave by the woman of the house, but her husband overruled her. Brad continued with his tirades when the husband was not home. Emma could do nothing about Brad staying in her house. She was trapped. I vowed I would get him out and knew that the answer would come soon. It did.

I consulted Randy Shaw on this issue, and he shared with me a technique that he had used once before. It was given to him by a Native American Indian spirit guide. The approach was to be used only in grave circumstances. It is, in effect, the nuke approach. It not only gets them out of the area, but also out of the whole vicinity. It was cautioned that it should be used only in the direst of circumstances. This was one of those circumstances. I was even under further resolve to remove Brad after what I heard the next day.

Emma and several other members of the household were in the house in the early afternoon. Brad was gone. As they were doing daily chores, a male shadow appeared in the living room. They described the outline of a man wearing a hat, but he was completely a dark shadow. No features on the face, no outline of clothing, only a dark shape that had the outlines of a human. Emma grabbed the children and ran screaming into her bedroom. Tara, her friend and woman of the house, confirmed the story the next day. I quickly caught up with Emma, and she confirmed it. I knew that now was the time to bring out the bomb.

That evening as the sun set, I went outside and performed the ceremony. It did not take long, but it felt powerful from my end. For the next two days, Brad acted increasingly hostile. Within two days, without explanation, he was gone. He completely left the area. It had worked. We were all elated. Brad was gone. We had hoped he had learned his lesson. For the moment, he had.

It was not long after Brad left that the whole story and motivation became clear. Emma had a trust fund back in England that was supposedly of a sizeable sum. Brad, it turned out, was quite a shady character. He was known for small crimes as well as smuggling drugs and weapons over the Canadian/U.S. border. He also was well practiced in the dark arts. He contrived a scheme to marry Emma and then kill her in hopes of inheriting her trust fund. This would have been all for naught, because later she discovered her father in England had absconded with the money, leaving her with nothing.

The story did not quite end with Brad leaving. A few weeks later, Emma left the area, healed of her cancer. She had a desire to go down to the Southwest and work with some Native American people there. Brad caught up with her and, on several occasions, beat her. She eventually got away from him by returning to England and changing her name. A couple of weeks after she returned, she visited a doctor to check on the status of her cancer. It was gone. She told the doctors how it had been accomplished. Amazed, they wanted to know more and gave me a call. Because of the time differences, I ended up leaving them a long and detailed message of the techniques I used, and had taught to Emma so she could work on herself, and let them know the sort of knowledge that I used was available to everyone. I lost track of Emma after that, but the time we spent together was one of great learning and experience for me.

The next story illustrates the issue of the spiritual world interacting with the physical world. It was done in a way that was perplexing to the client with whom we worked. However, as soon as it was explained to me, light instantly was shed on the situation, and it was soon remedied.

Enny and I had worked with Eileen and her three-year-old daughter, Maria, in the past, teaching Eileen Reiki and how to increase her intuitive abilities. One day we received a worried call from her. Her daughter had developed what appeared to be bruises all over her body. The bruises covered her from her shoulders and arms all the way down to her legs. It looked as though she had been pinched, or that there was some sub dermal bleeding occurring. They had been to the hospital for tests, but there was nothing medically that could account for her condition. It was getting to the point that Eileen was stressed out. Maria always was scared and crying, and there was a possibility that charges of abuse could occur.

As she was talking to me, the first thing that came into my head was "poltergeist." It was loud and clear. I did not want to voice my opinion right away, as I did not want to create any more fear within the family structure. I told Eileen that Enny and I would look into it and get back to her in the morning. After she hung up the phone, I went into a deep meditation to get more insight into what was going on in their household. I felt that the issues were spiritually driven and not medical and would require a spiritually based solution. I kept getting a strong message that there was a poltergeist in the house that was creating these marks on little Maria. When I returned home, I discussed the problem with Enny. That evening Enny went into a deep meditation and did a scan of Eileen's house. It did not take her long to discover who was creating the problems. Enny discovered a twelve-year-old girl named Cassie living in the house. Cassie was hiding in the back room. Enny talked with her, and the story of her life became apparent.

Cassie was a girl that lived in the 1950s and early '60s. Her father was a chronic alcoholic and an abuser. He physically abused his wife and family and sexually abused Cassie. One evening, he became intoxicated and went to Cassie. She resolved she was not going to allow her father to do it to her anymore. She refused, and her father became enraged. He smothered Cassie with a pillow. Cassie's father was so filled with remorse, he died several years later by drinking himself to death.

Cassie would not move into the light. She was afraid. She felt that if she did so, she would be judged and sent to hell. Because of this fear, she stayed around the apartment and the building, trapped. There, she found Maria and became her playmate. Maria was an open and psychic child. She communicated with Cassie easily and, because she saw Cassie only as another child playmate, was not afraid of her. They played together for several months until one day a fight ensued over some toys. Maria decided that she did not want to play with Cassie anymore. Cassie became angry and began to abuse Maria. She started to terrorize her in her sleep. In her waking hours, she would pinch and hurt her and push her down. It also was at this time Maria was having terrible nightmares and yelling and screaming in her sleep. She also began to become afraid at night, so Eileen would have to put her in bed and lie with her until she fell asleep.

Once Cassie was found out, she stepped forward and was sorry for everything that she had done. She still wanted to play with Maria and to be her friend. She wanted to make up for everything that she had done to her. She still wanted to stay in the house and be a part of the family. She liked the energies in the house and promised she would be good.

Once I had heard all the details about the incident, my first reaction was anger, but it quickly turned to compassion and a desire to help Cassie get out of the situation she was in. It was out of the question that Cassie remain in the household under current conditions. Maria was terrorized and, until Cassie moved into the light, she could not be trusted with Maria anymore. Beyond all that, once Eileen was told the whole story, she did not want Cassie anywhere near her house, her child, or her family. Eileen was understandably angry and also frightened. If she never saw Cassie again, it would have been too soon.

I removed Cassie from the house by putting up a protective barrier that she could not penetrate. Cassie was now homeless. There was a question whether we wanted her around our house, especially with our two young daughters. The last thing we needed was to bring her to us and have her do the same thing to Luna and Mesa. I placed a protective barrier around our place so that she could not enter. Our guides and angels had a different scenario for us, and one that we would have to get directly involved in to help Cassie move into the light.

Enny spent quite a bit of time talking with Cassie and attempting to get her to move on. Cassie's family had tried as well, especially her grandmother. However, she was stubborn and afraid and would not go. The morning after Cassie was removed from Eileen's house, and I had left to go to work, Cassie was allowed to enter our house by our gatekeeper spirit guides and angels. As Enny was sleeping, Cassie attempted to get into bed and sleep with her. Enny was in the half-awake, half-asleep state and was trying to get Cassie out of the bed and away from her. Once Enny realized what was happening, she fully awoke and told Cassie to get out of her bed. She did not want her sleeping with her or disturbing her. Cassie was reluctant to go, but Enny pushed her will on Cassie so that she had to leave. For Cassie, it was not that easy. Enny later told me the story and said as Cassie, dressed in a white, ethereally flowing nightgown, tried to leave the room, she rose up from the bed and floated to the ceiling. She dropped back down to the floor and then floated back up to the ceiling again. She did this several times. Enny had to help her out by opening a doorway for her to leave. Enny connected with her angel, Elizabeth, and asked why Cassie was allowed into the house when we expressly chose to keep her out. Elizabeth explained that Cassie really needed help. To facilitate that, Cassie was allowed to come into the house to express how important it was to continue to help her. Enny was completely protected throughout the whole incident, and it was allowed to happen for her higher good and growth.

When I returned home that evening, I was determined to help Cassie and get her moved into the light. I connected with Cassie at that point and explained to her that I would open a doorway for her. I told her that beyond that doorway was the love and light of God, and that there was nothing of which to be afraid. There were no tricks, no judgment, and that she needed to go as it was the normal process of being human. She finally agreed after Enny and I encased her in pure white God-centered light of unconditional love.

In beginning the process of opening a doorway to the other side, I brought in our angels and guides, as well as many other angels and light beings to help with the transition. I created the doorway for her to walk through. After the doorway was opened, I saw Cassie running toward it and into the shining white vortex of energy, her white nightgown flowing behind her. As this happened, I was touched and extremely happy. An abundance of pure love and light-centered energies touched me deeply. I was so happy that she had moved into the light. Her true healing would begin.

It also was at this time that we still were in contact with Eileen. She stated that things had begun to get better in the house, but she still felt a strong male presence. It was making her uncomfortable. Once again, Enny did a deep meditation and connected with Cassie's father. He was aware of all that had gone on with his daughter and was now ready to move into the light, too. He had been afraid of moving forward for the same reasons: fear of judgment and hell. That evening, I opened the gateway, and her father moved into the light. We asked Cassie if she was going to help her father, but she stated that she was not ready yet to interact with him and to fully forgive him for all that he had done to her. She was working on her own healing and, with time, would be able to forgive him.

After Cassie had left, the bruises began to heal, and no new ones appeared on Maria. Within a couple of weeks, the bruises had completely healed, but there was still some psychological work that needed to be done. Eileen spent a lot of time giving Maria extra love and attention to help her through her time of healing.

The ending of this situation was happy. Maria did suffer some emotional trauma from this incident, but Eileen was able to give lots of love to Maria so, in time, she was able to heal. This story is one that illustrates the importance of helping those spirits that are trapped between physicality and the higher realms. The more we can help these souls, the fewer the incidents will occur similar to the story of Maria, Eileen, and Cassie.

Once again, I don't want to create fear and alter the flow of interaction for our children with those in the spiritual realms. The interaction will occur on many different levels with our children, including dream state. We have found that some children who continue to have recurring nightmares may be visited by those who do not have their best interests at heart. Talking to them and finding out the details can go a long way in helping to discover if it is spiritual visitation or part of normal childhood fears. If it is determined that visitation is a possibility, it is important to find someone that can help in these matters. There are many qualified professionals able to do this work. We have found great peace for both the children and those creating the problems with loving and caring intervention.

This next story could have come from a novel by Clive Barker or Stephen King, but it did not. This was a real occurrence that happened to a client of ours shortly after the Cassie incident. This time we were even more ready to confront the situation that quickly unfolded before us.

It started with a phone call from a client, Chris. She had been having strong urges to hurt not only herself, but also her daughter. She had visions of picking up knives and stabbing her daughter, and had to stop herself from beating and hurting her. She had resisted putting her own hand in a blender or toaster. She had repeatedly stopped herself, but it was getting increasingly difficult. She feared she was going insane and would soon be spending her time in a mental institution. As I listened on the other end of the phone, I knew there was a dark presence that was trying to push its will on her. I immediately began to place white light barriers of protection around her, her daughter April, and the whole household. Enny and I then connected with the being that was the cause of these destructive energy patterns.

The entity in the house was a man, a serial killer. He had committed suicide two years before by hanging himself due to the internal torments that haunted him. He was a person that liked control and liked the control he had over his victims before he killed them. His deeds were known, but he never had been caught or been tied to the killings. He was a dark energy and enjoyed the mind control he had inflicted on others in his spiritual state. He had created the same scenario over and over again within the two years he had been in spirit form. Deep down he was a lonely and unloved person, which ultimately had driven him to do the acts while he was alive on earth. As he crossed over into spirit, his powers and his anonymity increased tenfold.

Enny and I knew we could not just push him away from Chris and protect her from him. We had to help him move into the light so he would not continue to wander the planet, doing this to others. The big question was whether he would want to go. We knew we could protect ourselves from him, so we moved forward to help him find the peace and healing he needed.

We connected with him and found out that he was terrified of moving into the light. He felt because of all that he had done and all the murder and suffering he had caused, that he surely would be condemned to hell and everlasting torment. This was from his spiritual beliefs and upbringing. We let him know that the Creator loved him no matter what he had done. In order to set things right, he needed to stop what he was doing, move into the light of unconditional love, and begin his own process of self-forgiveness and healing. He still was uncertain about what we proposed. We told him to look at what we were doing at Moonglow and to see how many people were moving into the light nightly. We called upon our angels and guides to talk with him and to let him see that there was only love waiting for him, not torment as he expected.

While he was deciding what to do, he was brought before us so that we could have direct interaction with him. Our angels, Elizabeth and Susan, for our protection, bound him in a white light. We spoke to him one last time in his current situation. We sent him copious amounts of love and light and let him know there was a whole universe waiting for him to explore. We let him know that in a healed state, he had much to offer. It was this continued bombardment of positive and unconditional love that finally helped him to make the decision to move into the light, to heal, and to be loved. That evening, escorted by angels, he began his journey. Enny connected with him again shortly after, and he affirmed that he was doing much better. He said he was extremely sorry for all the hurt and pain he had caused. He understood that he would have to karmically atone for what he had done. He accepted his responsibility. He said he would do whatever it took to make things right. Enny and I know that it is between him and God. Things will be put back into balance.

A month later, Enny and I were doing a Reiki session with Chris. She had healed considerably, and her situation was much better. She was looking for guidance on how to protect herself from future attacks. She also wanted to know how to use her personal power to say no to any further intrusions into her life. As part of her learning process, we consulted with a trusted spiritual advisor who also helped her to find her internal power to say no. Each one of us has this power to say no to negativity and no to darker, more self-centered and selfish spiritual energies that may want to intrude upon our lives. If we say yes to the unconditional loving energies that abound throughout the universe and surround ourselves with these energies, then there is nothing negative that can penetrate that.

What exactly are the ways to protect ourselves from these types of attacks? An Internet or book search will produce many, each unique in their own way. I believe the single most powerful tool for protection is our own thoughts and intentions. Objects of power are used, such as stones, talismans, herbs, and incantations, but using the mind to focus light and love around our environment and ourselves is more powerful. Physical objects are useful to ground our intentions, but they must come from within us to make them effective. When I worked with Emma, Maria, and Chris, the first thing I did was to wrap them in the unconditional loving light of the Creator. There is nothing more powerful than this energy. I did this through intention. Anyone can do it. The more it is practiced, the stronger the protection will become.

A simple method is to begin with yourself. Stand in front of a full-length mirror. If you do not have one, then envision yourself standing facing you. Take a few deep breaths and intention pure white or golden light entering the top of your head, down your spine, then your arms, and into your hands. With this energy at the tips of your fingers, start at the top of your head and wrap yourself up in this energy. Remember to go three hundred sixty degrees around your body and under your feet. Encase yourself in this white or golden light. In your mind, see this energy surrounding you. While doing this, you may feel a slight tingling sensation in your hands, down your spine, or around your body. You are moving energy!

Another powerful way to intention and aid in the flow of protection is through prayer. Many ascended masters and angels exist to help us stay protected from spiritual harm. In the Westernized world, the most prevalent is Jesus. Drawing Christ energy around you, your loved ones, and your household is a very powerful channel for protection. The power of Mary also is similar in its effects. Other Christians like to use the power of saints. This, too, can be a way to bring powerful protective energies into your life.

Others in the world look to Krishna as their path to the divine light. Using the protective power of Krishna and other Hindu saints can channel the protective life force energies of the Creator all around you. Mohammed, Buddha, and other ascended masters are all available when asked. Archangels and other angels also are called upon to help aid in psychic and spiritual protection. They key is to call upon those energies that you resonate to the most. The Creator has given us a vast array of powerful choices to use to keep us safe when growing spiritually and emotionally. Through the power of prayer and intention, we become the lightning rod to ground those energies. Surrounding ourselves in this light will keep us interacting with only those guides, angels, and loved ones that are present for our highest good.

These techniques also can be used when surrounding or protecting children. As stated earlier in this book it is encouraged to have children interact on a higher spiritual level. Using the power of prayer and intention is a good way to protect the living and sleeping areas of children. In the physical action of grounding the energies, parents can feel much more safe and secure that our children are interacting with those that love and care for them

This encasement of energy is powerful, but needs to be refined over time. A more effective and longer lasting way to keep negativity from you is to shine from the inside out. Shining white or golden love energies constantly will create an almost impenetrable barrier around you that never needs maintenance or work. This can be accomplished through one simple action, LOVE. Begin by loving yourself. Know that whatever you have done in your life is in the past. Recognize that you are a being of light, residing in an imperfect physical body and society. We all make decisions that take us from our life's purpose and God's desire of our growth toward perfection. Love heals all and is the source of the most powerful protection.

11

Following a Higher Spiritual Path

All the information that I have shared in this book is meant to help each person reading it either to begin or refine a path that helps to discover a higher purpose and sense of being. This path of higher spirituality is one of many rewards. It also can seriously change our view of reality and what we have perceived throughout much of our lives as "The Truth." It also can change the way others view us and the way we begin to view others. So I want to impart some wisdom that I have accrued that may help this path be easier. I feel it is always better to learn from others' experiences than to go through some of the harder lessons if we do not have to. I am addressing this chapter to "YOU" directly because you are the one that is reading this and the one that likely will be following or are following a more energetic path.

First of all, following a higher spiritual path will change your energetic nature. By this I mean that as you search for your own highest truth, your physical, auric, and emotional bodies will change. This will manifest in spontaneous emotional releases as healing occurs, weight loss or gain, a "spacey" or ungrounded feeling, or other perceived changes. Activities need to be done to help maintain the balance through the tumultuous times that are ahead. This also holds true for those of you who already are following this path and have felt these changes but are unsure what to do to help bring about balance. I do not advocate attempting drastic changes, as they never seem to stick. Integrating a healthier lifestyle on a daily basis will dramatically help in staying grounded and keeping the body nourished on all levels.

Meditation is one of the main activities that should become integrated into your life. Meditation is the single most powerful undertaking with which you can start. It helps to bring the changes that are occurring into greater focus, as well as keep the body, mind, and spirit in balance. There are many different forms of meditation and, in this day and age, getting access to information about meditation is easy. Take some time to try out different methods until you find one that works for you. Typically silence and breathing are the key to successful meditation. The silence will help to quiet the mind, and the breathing will help to reenergize the body. It may take some time before you are able to quiet your mind or sit still long enough to begin to feel the effects. You still will derive benefits even if you can sit quietly and breathe for five minutes. You can increase that time as you are able. Quieting the mind in our busy lives can be a challenge. It is like trying to cut your way through a wall of thorns but, believe me, on the other side of that wall is serenity and a space that will be easier to get to each time. If you are following a shamanic path and desire to work with the spiritual realms, then within this stillness can be the perfect opportunity to open the doors to communication. Over time, this communication will occur without the need for a meditative state. The meditative state then will become a sanctuary from all outside influences including spiritual in nature. The key is to stick with it, increase your time, and before you know it, you will find your own space of serenity and peace. It is a beautiful thing.

Meditation techniques are fairly simple, but mastering quieting the mind can take a little longer. A simple technique to use starts with posture. Lying down and attempting to meditate will often end in sleep. This is not the desired result. The back should remain straight and unsupported. Sitting on a bench or stool with no back to rest upon is ideal. For those with back pain or back issues, a chair with a straight back will work best. Meditation should not be limited to posture only, so for anyone with an illness that makes it difficult to sit with your back straight, a position of comfort is sufficient. Close your eyes and concentrate on your breathing. A good method to regulate breathing is to begin with a count of four. Breathe in counting to four; breathe out counting to four. Keep these counts regulated. Breathe deeply so the air reaches the lower lung through moving the diaphragm and not the chest. The body will become oxygenated, and the energy will begin to flow through the body. Try to sit for at least five minutes and increase it as you practice. Thoughts will continually enter your mind. The key is to not allow yourself to follow them to conclusion or begin to stray with other thoughts deriving from the original. Acknowledge the thoughts, but bring your concentration back to your breathing. Stay centered on the action of the breath going in and out of your lungs. Let all worries and need for mental stimulation slip away. Try not to continually monitor your progress of time by opening your eyes and looking at a clock. Let the time flow. Keep yourself concentrated on the present. As your ability to stay centered on meditation increases, you may find yourself dozing off. This is common, and after practicing no longer occurs. During the time you are able to meditate, let yourself know there is nothing more important than the action you are undertaking. The benefits of your actions will be returned tenfold. You will feel more centered, energized, and relaxed.

Connecting to the spiritual realms becomes much easier when the mind is quieted of its distractions. In the beginning, it is hard to discern information being received that is spiritual in knowledge and that which is egoic in nature. The information that is given will sound like your own voice in your head. Flashes of information may come through, and even quick visions. Continue to work with those, and begin to trust what is given to you. Spiritual activity is often seen through the third eye or the psychic centers rather than the physical eye. While meditating, you may experience flashes of light or colored lights moving behind the eyes. This is the beginning of perception of spiritual activity. Dreams also are an active place for spiritual activity to begin. If a being comes to your dreams that seems familiar and gives you messages, this is most likely one of your spirit guides communicating with you. If someone that has crossed over comes to you and talks to you or relays messages, this also is spiritual activity. Sitting quietly with a pen and paper and writing down all the thoughts that come into your head is called *autowriting* and is a slower, but powerful, way to begin to connect to the spiritual realms. Use meditation to remove the egoic chatter of the mind. Then let information flow to you. Trust what you see, hear, smell, or feel. Let your fear down as it will make it much more difficult for spiritual messages to get through when you have unneeded walls and protection placed around yourself. Intention that the protection you have around you will allow those experiences in that are love and light-oriented and are for your highest good. Stones such as amethyst and quartz crystal held in the hand during these activities can help to amplify your ability to receive messages. The more you practice and work on receiving spiritual information, the more intuitive and accurate you will become.

A good example of letting information flow happened when I was working with a client, Robin, connecting her to her family members that had crossed over. I connected to her grandfather and gave a lot of information that pertained to him that was familiar to her. He had emigrated from Europe and had worked on the railroad for a number of years. At one point, I kept seeing him putting a duck in the bathtub. I asked her about it, and she had no idea of the meaning. After the session, she called her mother and asked her about it. She stated that he liked to eat duck soup so would go out, get a live duck, and keep it in the tub until it was ready to be eaten. Because I was open and just let it flow, I was able to relay accurate and amusing information. This keeps the session from being generic such as, "Your loved one misses you" or "They love you." The more accurate the information is, the better the experience for all those involved.

The second area of importance is diet. Remember that everything is made of energy and vibrates at different frequencies. In addition to taxing the liver, heart, and kidneys, processed foods high in sugar, salt, and empty calories vibrate at a much lower level than fresh organic foods. Your body is more thankful for the organic foods. Does this mean you should immediately stop eating all lower energy foods and switch to an organic macrobiotic diet? That would not be practical. For most of us, a change in diet must be accomplished from not only changes in our actions, but also changes in our thoughts and the way we see ourselves. Your diet is a direct reflection of how you feel about yourself. Your body is happier with high-energy organic foods. Think about the consequences of physically picking up the food in front of you and putting it into your body's system. This will help you begin to make better choices. The three-meat pizza with all the trimmings appeals to your ego and need for instant gratification, not to your body, which must continue processing that food long after you have eaten it. The human body is a marvelous system which, given normal health, can withstand a certain amount of punishment. As your energy and vibration levels change, so too will your body's ability to assimilate certain types of foods as well as other substances such as tobacco and alcohol. Highly refined foods, alcohol, and tobacco will do greater damage to the body as your energy levels rise. Thus, certain foods or substances may begin to make you sick after ingesting or inhaling them. Small amounts of alcohol may cause headaches, and caffeine may begin to make you feel nervous and jumpy. Meat may begin to be unappealing, and the process of eating animal flesh may not have the same allure as it once did. The quicker you can phase these out of your life, the quicker you will grow as a person and the happier your body will be.

Making the gradual changes may be challenging, but they can be accomplished. If you are a smoker, begin by smoking fewer cigarettes each day. Instead of having two or three drinks after coming home from work to release stress, try exercising, meditating, or doing something else you enjoy. If you eat many high-sugar foods, gradually substitute natural items such as fresh fruits. These changes will be easier for some than for others, but remember that you are never alone in your quest for healthy changes. Your spirit guides and angels are always there to help. Ask for spirit guides that can help you on your quest. Surround yourself with the white light of healing and protection as well as strength to get you through the times when the desire for self-destructive behavior is strongest. Remember it is the ego that wants to be fed, like a little child. Find the strength within to help quell that child. There will be times when you are unable, or even unwilling, to make the correct choices. Keep trying. Being conscious of the desire to change is important. Congratulate yourself on the effort, even if you are not wholly successful. Avoid self-recrimination and feelings of guilt during the times when you are unable to overcome the ego. Keep in mind that the ego has been a powerful part of your life for many years. It will take time to overcome some of the more destructive habits you have acquired. Remember also that change is part of the journey of discovery. As you work to overcome your own bad habits, you can relay information to others, helping them on their journey.

My own experiences mirror these concepts well. Since I was about nineteen years old, I have struggled between loving lower energy foods and having a diet that was moderately healthy. This included loving pizzas and burgers, but also trying to stay balanced by eating fresh foods. I also liked to drink alcohol. Not so much for the effects, although throughout my college years I did like to stay out late and drink with the best of them. As I got older my pallet changed, and I liked to drink the handcrafted micro brews. When I began this path, I kept drinking alcohol and kept eating lower energy foods. That soon ended as I began to get pains in my liver and kidneys. The energy changes for me were quite dramatic and fast, and my body could no longer handle drinking alcohol or eating foods high in sugars such as ice cream. I loved both dearly, but that was my egoic gratification needing its fix. I knew I had to change my diet as well as quit drinking for good, or my health would deteriorate with my growth and development. I called in all my guides and angels and asked them for help with my decision to quit drinking and to keep away from foods high in sugar. The next day I went out, exercised hard and, when I was finished, I had no more cravings for alcohol. I completely quit drinking that day and have not had cravings for alcohol since. It took longer to rid myself of the need for sugar, but I have now integrated natural sugars such as fruit into my diet, and I keep them in balance. I also have cut out all beef and pork. On the rare occasion when I eat meat, I try to be sure it is organic. As a result of these changes, I lost twenty-five pounds and felt much healthier. I no longer have liver and kidney problems, but I know they would return if I reverted to my previous lifestyle.

As you begin to make changes in your lifestyle and habits, you, too, will find that as your energy levels increase you may experience significant weight loss. If we look back at the great masters who have followed a God-realized path, their diets were simple and consisted in large measure of fresh vegetables and fruit. They loved themselves as they loved God, and they recognized that their bodies were a reflection of God's love for them. By treating their bodies well, they showed reverence for themselves as well as the Creator. Instead of living to eat, we should eat to live.

Thirdly, exercise is essential if you are following a higher path. Helping others to heal through energy work will deplete your body of energy. You will have to cleanse yourself of the negative releases from those with whom you are working. Different types of releases occur whenever a person begins or is working on the healing process. Two of the most common are emotional release and the release of blocked energy. As a practitioner, you may inadvertently absorb some of these negative energies. This will occur whether you choose to work with clients professionally or with friends and family. The best and healthiest way to release not only stress energies that accumulate through daily life, but also the negative energies absorbed through working with others, is exercise.

Each person has his or her own interest for physical activity. Whatever you are interested in or able to do, it is important that you do it. If you are already on a daily exercise routine, congratulations, you already have integrated this step into your life. However, for those of you who have not, it is important that you start. Connecting to the spiritual realms can be draining and unbalancing. It can be so much so that if energy is not replaced, then physical illnesses can occur. Exercising will replenish the vital life force energies into the body. No matter what level of activity you are able to undertake, do it. If you are a runner, run. If you like basketball, skiing, aerobics, or any other forms of activity, try to do it several times a week or after channeling or energy healing. If you are able to exercise before working with spiritual energies, you will find that the channels will be more open and clear. Exercise also is helpful before meditation. Light exercise such as stretching and yoga can energize the body, which will help quiet the mind. Any great master that has written about meditation or developed a regimen also has included exercise as part of it. There also are forms of exercise and breathing that are directly focused on energizing the body. Yoga, Tai Chi, Chi Gong, and many others are available to help maintain good health.

Another area to focus on is the concept of giving and receiving. Giving of and to ourselves is a concept that has been taught by great masters through the millennium. One of the central focuses in the Bible, Koran, and Hindu Vedas revolve around giving unselfishly to others, particularly those in need. In doing this, we begin a cycle of abundance that can help us greatly in our lives. This is a central focus that can be part of your own spiritual development. As we give, so shall we receive. However, giving for the sake of thinking that we will receive in return often does not work. Remember, the path you are on is one of God-centered unconditional love and light. As you allow more of God's light into your heart, so shall you want to give of yourself for others. As this cycle of abundance begins, you will be amazed at the gifts you will receive in return. One of the first and most apparent that you will find is the abundance of knowledge that will begin to come your way. You will find yourself being in the right place at the right time to receive information that will be in your best interest. Physical gifts will be become abundant as well. These will come your way from others that you have helped. It is important that you receive these gifts. It keeps the energy of the cycle of abundance flowing. If you refuse these gifts, then you are sending a message to the universe that you do not want to receive, and the abundance will begin to recede. As you like to give, so shall others.

If you are a person who has a hard time giving to others and is looking to follow a spiritual or healing path to receive only then, once again, you will find this cycle incomplete. It is important to heal the issues of attachment to physical items. If you have many unused items in your house that you are saving for a "rainy day" that never seems to come, take some of them and give them to someone who may need them more. Giving from the heart is one of the most powerful actions you can do to help with your growth and development. Unfortunately, in our Westernized societies, money and itemized wealth is predominant, taking the place of sharing and helping to equalize the disparities among people that may have trouble manifesting abundance in their own lives. Help to heal your own heart center by finding items that you own that are not used anymore and give them to someone or an organization that will be able to use them more fully. Even better, find objects you hold dear and give them to someone who needs them more. In doing so, you are practicing a powerful activity that will have great repercussions for you on many levels. The more you can become unattached from physical items, the greater your own growth will be.

Your enlightenment will hasten if you can find someone with whom to share your experiences. Growth is often dramatic, and you will want to let others know of your progress. Whom you choose to share the information with can either help or hinder you. It is important to share your questions and challenges with somebody who can answer them or at least help you to explore them together. Sometimes family members are not ones that may be the most supportive, particularly if they hold strong dogmatic religious viewpoints. Energy healing and spiritual communication is viewed by many conservative religious persons to be satanically oriented or leads the way down dark and evil paths. It is actually the exact opposite. Spiritual growth and knowledge will bring you closer to God and light-oriented activity. However, this fear can be deep seated and destructive toward those that do not fit a certain mold or frame. If such people surround you, then it may be best to share your experiences with a different group. I do not advocate secrecy or lying, but sometimes keeping your experiences to yourself can be the best course of action.

Each person must make their own choices as to how much information they share with others. You also may find yourself, as many others have, leading a double life. How much you share with your spouse, children, parents, and friends is up to you. Some people have supportive environments in which to grow. Others find the path difficult with spouses not understanding their path, which may lead to strains in the relationship. It is important for longevity that this growth occurs for both involved in the marriage. I have seen divorces occur because of dramatic changes in one person while fear and judgment were the response of the other.

Many groups exist to help support others through the growth process. Reiki sharings are a good place to start. Another may be spiritualist or nondenominational churches. This is a supportive environment where people gather to share healing and experiences. If these are not found near you, many online communities are available to get this support. In our modern day society, time and space are no longer a barrier to growth. As you search for these communities, the answers will come to you. Remember that your spirit guides and angels are with you to help you through your search.

Many teachers are available that can help you find answers to the questions coming to the forefront of your life. Find one with which you feel comfortable. A good judge of a teacher is if they are living what they preach. Whatever skill or service you are seeking, take the time to ask questions of the practitioner. Shop around to see what other teachers may be available to help you. Just because a person calls himself or herself a teacher does not mean you may resonate to that person's particular teaching style or personality. Price also is not an indicator of how good a person is. Some people have other forms of income that pay the basic bills and choose to charge less. Others are on a karmic path to charge little to help more people. However, also bear in mind that some people make the spiritual path their only form of survival. Find a teacher that you can afford and one to whom you resonate. In doing so, your journey will be more enjoyable and fruitful.

In this book, I have shared many of my experiences and knowledge that I have gained through my life. Some of you reading this book will be skeptical. That is OK. The key is that some new ideas have been given to you to think about. For others, these may be new ideas to take hold of and begin your own journey into discovery. The truth that you will find will be unique to you. Much of what you have read is meant to be a guide to forge your own path. For many more, this may be confirmation of experiences that already have happened to you. Wherever you are in your life, know that there is always much more waiting out there to be discovered. The expressions of God's love are as varied as our own imaginations. Much is happening in the vast universe that we have yet to discover. Do not worry or be afraid. We have eternity not only to discover what lies beyond our own earthly reality, but also to discover our true selves. In our growth, each one of us comes closer to returning to God's waiting and unconditionally loving arms.

Bibliography

Andrews, Ted. *How to Meet and Work with Spirit Guides.* Llewellyn Publications, St. Paul, 1992

Andrews, Ted *How to Uncover Your Past Lives.* Llewellyn Publications, St. Paul, 1991

Andrews, Ted *How to Do Psychic Readings Through Touch.* Llewellyn Publications, St. Paul, 1994

Andrews, Ted *How to Heal with Color.* Llewellyn Publications, St. Paul, 1992

Andrews, Ted *The Healer's Manual.* Llewellyn Publications, St. Paul 1993

Addams, Jane *Twenty Years At Hull-House,* The Macmillan Company, New York, 1966

Yogananda, *Autobiography of a Yogi.* New York: Philosophical Library, 1946

0-595-32796-6

Printed in the United States
37987LVS00006B/220-318